SOFTBALL
RULES IN PICTURES

G. JACOBS McCRORY

TECHNICAL CONSULTANTS:

DON E. PORTER
Executive Director, Amateur Softball Association of America

GEORGE T. CRON
Chairman, International Joint Rules Committee on Softball

TOM MASON
I.J.R.C. Interpreter/National ASA Umpire-in-Chief

CHARLES E. KING

ILLUSTRATOR:

HARRY SINGLETON

GROSSET & DUNLAP

A Filmways Company

PUBLISHERS   NEW YORK

The set of six filmstrips in color entitled **SOFTBALL RULES AND OFFICIATING** from which this book was made is available from School Film Service, 171 Elton Road, Garden City, New York 11530

Excerpts from the **OFFICIAL SOFTBALL RULES,** under copyright by the International Joint Rules on Softball (revised 1977), reprinted with permission.

DEDICATION

To my team: John, Claude Ray, George, Charlie,

Karl, Ron, Jim, Robert and Harry.

Contents

FOREWORD

This book is intended for the softball player, manager and umpire. It presents the rules in a simple, easy-to-understand picture form and is a stimulating and enjoyable way to learn the softball rules.

To the player and the manager, a thorough knowledge of the rules is an asset. To the umpire, a thorough knowledge of the rules is a necessity. New umpires will find *Softball Rules in Pictures* to be an easy method of rule study. The visual presentation of the rules, together with the short and concise captions, makes possible a clearer and deeper understanding of the sometimes technical and complicated official rules. For this reason, the veteran umpire will see the book as a helpful, preseason refresher course. A section on umpire positioning provides insight into the improved positioning techniques now used by umpires nationally.

A complete set of Slow Pitch and Fast Pitch rules can be found in the *Official Guide* published by the Amateur Softball Association of America, 2801 N.E. 50th Street, Oklahoma 73111.

TOM MASON
National ASA Umpire-In-Chief

Fast Pitch

SOFTBALL

- The game is played by two teams of nine players each.

- It is played with a bat and ball on a diamond - shaped field.

- The object of the game is to score runs for your team.

In Slow Pitch there are 10 players on a team.

It is recommended that all players - as well as umpires - be examined by a doctor.

THE PLAYING FIELD

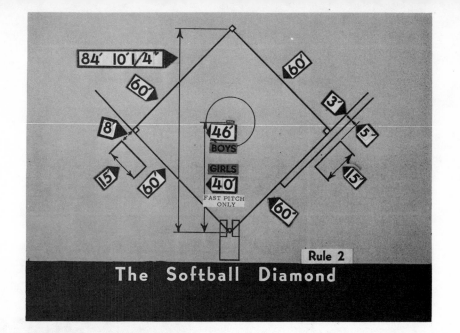

84' 10 1/4"

60'

60'

3'

8'

5'

46' BOYS

GIRLS 40'

FAST PITCH ONLY

15'

15'

60'

60'

Rule 2

The Softball Diamond

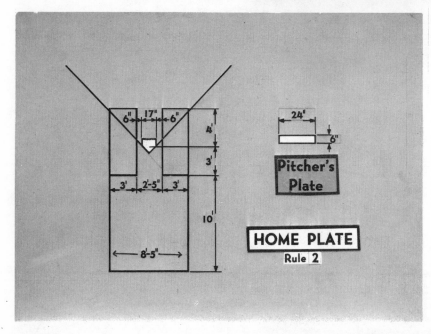

6" 17" 6"

4'

3'

24"

6"

3' 2'-5" 3'

10'

Pitcher's Plate

8'-5"

HOME PLATE

Rule 2

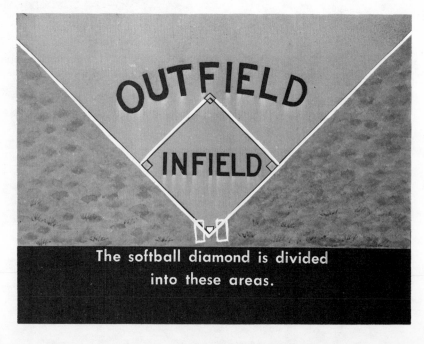

OUTFIELD

INFIELD

The softball diamond is divided into these areas.

8

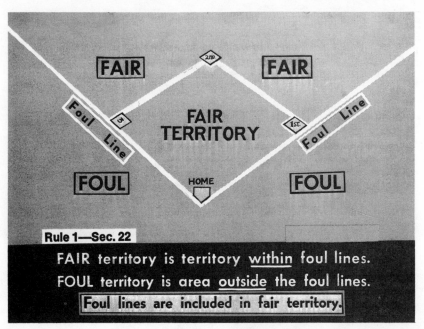

FAIR

FAIR

Foul Line

FAIR
TERRITORY

Foul Line

FOUL

FOUL

HOME

Rule 1—Sec. 22

FAIR territory is territory <u>within</u> foul lines.
FOUL territory is area <u>outside</u> the foul lines.

Foul lines are included in fair territory.

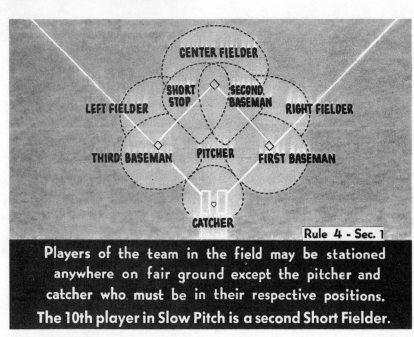

CENTER FIELDER

SHORT
STOP

SECOND
BASEMAN

LEFT FIELDER

RIGHT FIELDER

THIRD BASEMAN

PITCHER

FIRST BASEMAN

CATCHER

Rule 4 - Sec. 1

Players of the team in the field may be stationed
anywhere on fair ground except the pitcher and
catcher who must be in their respective positions.
The 10th player in Slow Pitch is a second Short Fielder.

EQUIPMENT

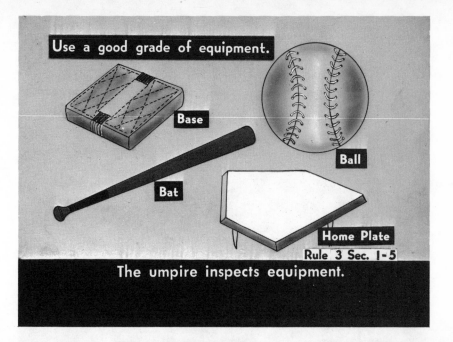

Use a good grade of equipment.

Base

Ball

Bat

Home Plate

Rule 3 Sec. 1-5

The umpire inspects equipment.

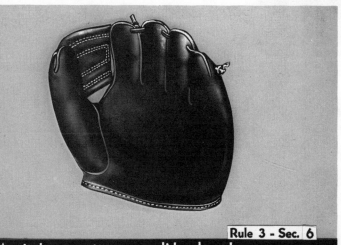

Rule 3 - Sec. 6

A pitcher must use a solid color glove,
other than white or gray.

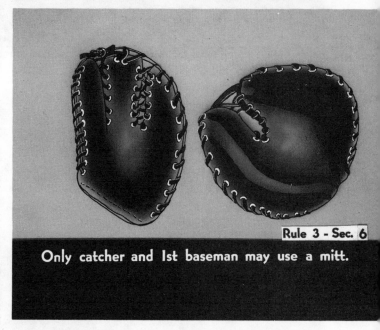

Rule 3 - Sec. 6

Only catcher and 1st baseman may use a mitt.

Both the catcher and umpire wear
a mask and a chest protector.
Fast Pitch Only

Captains toss a coin for choice of innings at the beginning of the game, - unless otherwise decided.

The choice of first or last bat in the inning shall be decided by the toss of a coin unless stated otherwise before the game.   Rule 5–Sec. 1

The Defensive team is in the field.
The team at bat is the Offensive Team.

Rule 5 - Sec. 5

One run shall be scored each time a runner legally touches 1st, 2nd, 3rd bases and home plate before the 3rd out of the inning.

Rule 1—Sec. 36

An INNING is that portion of a game within which teams alternate on offence and defense and in which there are 3 outs for each team.

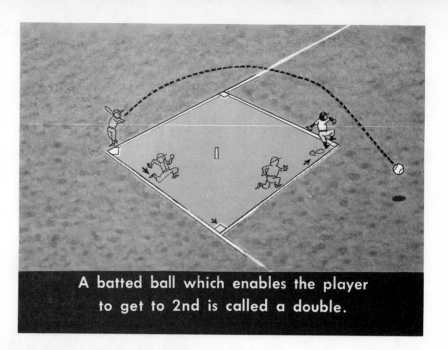

A batted ball which enables the player
to get to 2nd is called a double.

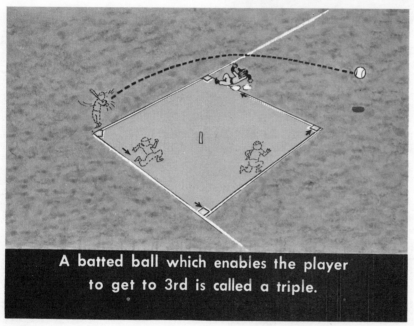

A batted ball which enables the player
to get to 3rd is called a triple.

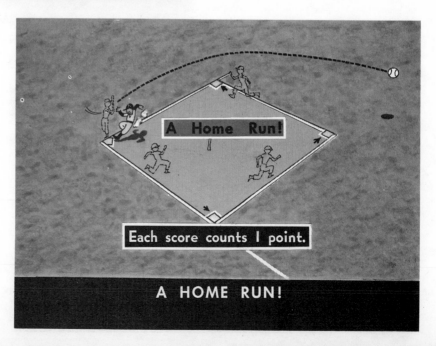

A Home Run!

Each score counts 1 point.

A HOME RUN!

The batter completes his turn at bat when
he becomes a baserunner or --- is out.

A FAIR BALL MUST:

1. Settle in fair territory between first
   and third bases - - or

2. Bounce past third or first base
   in fair territory - - or

3. Bounce over first or third base - - or

4. First fall fair beyond 1st or 3rd
   on a fly ball.

Rule 1—Sec. 11

A Bunt is a batted ball not swung at, but
intentionally met with the bat and tapped
slowly within the infield.

In Slow Pitch the bunt is illegal.

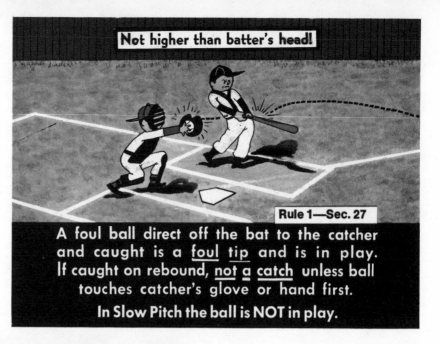

Not higher than batter's head!

Rule 1—Sec. 27

A foul ball direct off the bat to the catcher
and caught is a <u>foul</u> tip and is in play.
If caught on rebound, <u>not</u> <u>a</u> <u>catch</u> unless ball
touches catcher's glove or hand first.

In Slow Pitch the ball is NOT in play.

**Players must be on
1 & 2 or all 3 bases.**

THERE ARE LESS
THAN 2 OUTS.

Rule 1—Sec. 35

An Infield Fly is a fair fly ball, other than a
line drive or attempted bunt which can be
caught by an infielder with ordinary effort.

"A good guide" to determine if infield fly:
Could fielder be facing toward batter when
making catch? Here NOT an infield fly.

On a dead ball the play is stopped.
No one can advance to bases.
- - unless awarded a base.

No one can be put out.

All substitutions should be reported
to the umpire
The substitute shall take the position of
the player whom he is replacing.
Rule 4 - Sec. 3a

APPEAL PLAYS

An appeal is an act of the defensive
team in claiming a violation of the
rules by the offensive team.

An Appeal must be made to
the umpire by defensive player
before next pitch to batter
-- be it legal or illegal --
--or before all infielders have left field.

An appeal play

Rule 8—Sec. 9g

Failing to return to 1st base immediately
after overrunning or oversliding.

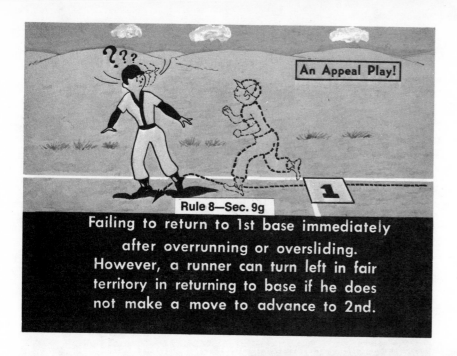

An Appeal Play!

Rule 8—Sec. 9g

Failing to return to 1st base immediately after overrunning or oversliding. However, a runner can turn left in fair territory in returning to base if he does not make a move to advance to 2nd.

An Appeal Play!

Rule 8—Sec. 8g

If a runner misses a base, he may be put out by a fielder touching the base with the ball before the runner retags the base.

An Appeal Play!

Rule 8—Sec. 8i

The runner is out if he overslides home plate - misses it - and the plate is tagged by a fielder before the runner returns.

Each score counts 1 point.

Rule 5 - Sec. 5

Runs score if appeal play for third out
is behind the runner.

These runs score.

Rule 5 - Sec. 7

If a preceding runner "misses" a base, it does
not affect the baserunners behind him, whether
put out or not, unless it's the 3rd out.

3 OUTS

Rule 5 - Sec. 6 b

RUNS DO NOT SCORE

If any other runner is put out
by a force out for 3rd out.

3 OUTS!

Rule 8—Sec. 7d   Rule 5 - Sec. 6 a

Run shall not count if the 3rd out was
made because the batter failed to reach 1st.

RUNS DO NOT SCORE

Rule 5 Sec. 7

If a preceding runner is the 3rd
out on an appeal play.

vs ———

Players	Pos.	1	2	3	4	5	6	7
Quane	3	6-4 ①/W	① F4	◆ E6		① 5-3		
Sub.								
Smith	6	◆ F.C.	◆ ≡	⌐ ꞊		② 2-3		
Sub.								
Adair	4	◆ ꞊	② K2	② F5		6-4 ②/-		
Sub.								
Unger	7	◆ E9	◆ ꞊	③ K2		/F.C.		
Sub.								
Sewell 3	8	⌐ -	/ -		① 2-3			
Sub Nelson 8	8							
Celander	2	/-3 ①/SH	③ K2					
Sub.								
Gauld	5	/E2		◆ ꞊	/ -			
Sub.								
Jones	9	③ K2		◆ ꞊	③ K2			
Sub.								
Lewis	1		◆ W	① F3		◆ ꞊		
Sub.								
Sub.								
Sub.								
Summary	Runs Hits	3/2	3/3	3/3	0/1	1/1	/	/

Umpire _____   Scorer _____
Umpire _____   Date _____

K	Strike Out
/W	Walk
F -	Fly Out
E	Error
K, E$_2$	Missed 3rd Strike
F. C.	Fielder's Choice
	in making a put-out
S.H.	Sacrifice Play
②	No. of Outs (circled)
1 -	One Base Hit
﹥ ꞊	Two Base Hit
˄ ☰	Three Base Hit
◆ ☰	Home Run
◆	Completed Run
□	End of Inning

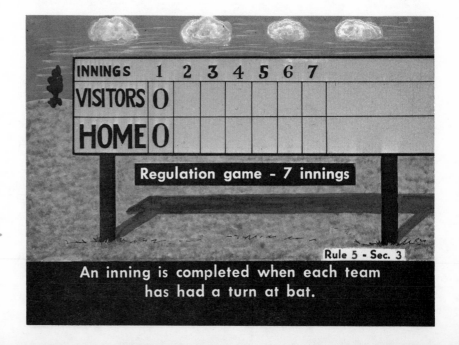

INNINGS 1 2 3 4 5 6 7
VISITORS 0
HOME 0

Regulation game - 7 innings

Rule 5 - Sec. 3

An inning is completed when each team
has had a turn at bat.

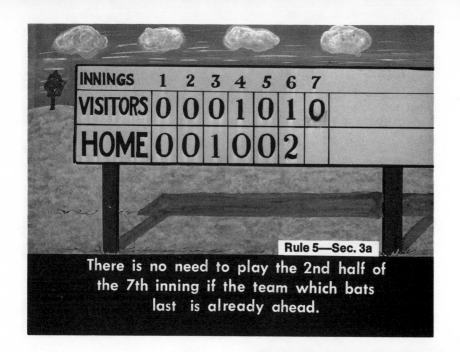

INNINGS	1	2	3	4	5	6	7
VISITORS	0	0	0	1	0	1	0
HOME	0	0	1	0	0	2	

Rule 5—Sec. 3a

There is no need to play the 2nd half of the 7th inning if the team which bats last is already ahead.

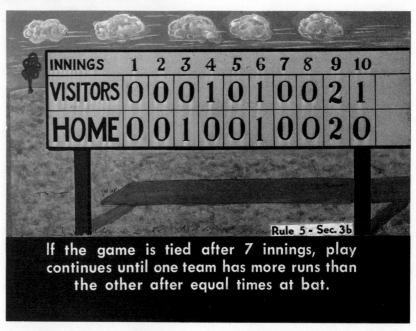

INNINGS	1	2	3	4	5	6	7	8	9	10
VISITORS	0	0	0	1	0	1	0	0	2	1
HOME	0	0	1	0	0	1	0	0	2	0

Rule 5 - Sec. 3b

If the game is tied after 7 innings, play continues until one team has more runs than the other after equal times at bat.

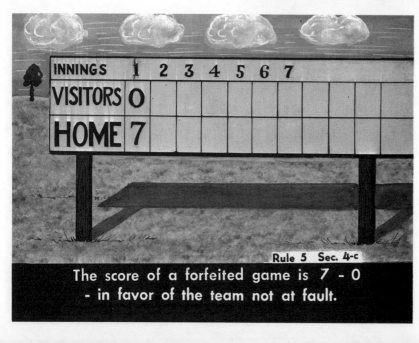

INNINGS	1	2	3	4	5	6	7
VISITORS	0						
HOME	7						

Rule 5   Sec. 4-c

The score of a forfeited game is 7 - 0 - in favor of the team not at fault.

THE PITCHER

A valuable training aid for pitchers is a strike zone target.

These are the RULES
the pitcher must follow.

Failure to follow these rules will result in an illegal pitch.

The penalty for an illegal pitch is a ball being called on the batter and any baserunner may advance one base.

In Slow Pitch the runner does not advance on an illegal pitch—the ball is dead.

Rule 6 - Sec. 1
Rule 1—Sec. 47

To begin play - the umpire calls "Play Ball" while the pitcher is in pitching position.

In Slow Pitch only one foot must be in contact with the pitching rubber.

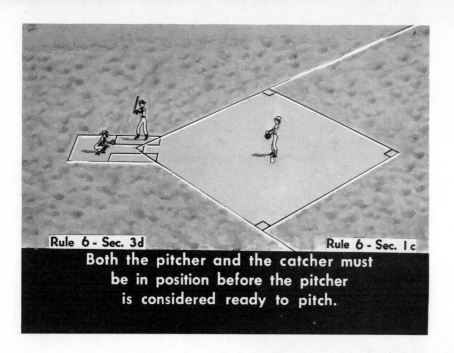

Rule 6 - Sec. 3d   Rule 6 - Sec. 1c

Both the pitcher and the catcher must
be in position before the pitcher
is considered ready to pitch.

Rule 6 - Sec. 1c

The catcher must be <u>inside</u> the catcher's box.

Ball is alive!

Rule 6 - Sec. 1a

The pitcher must stand squarely facing
the batter.

A ball is called for each illegal pitch.

Rule 6 - Sec. 1 a &b

The pitcher must have both feet in contact
with the pitcher's plate, come to a full stop
with the ball held in both hands, for at least
two seconds before starting his windup.
Only ONE foot must touch the pitching rubber
in Slow Pitch.

Rule 6 - Sec. 1b

It is an illegal pitch to hold the ball
for more than 20 seconds.

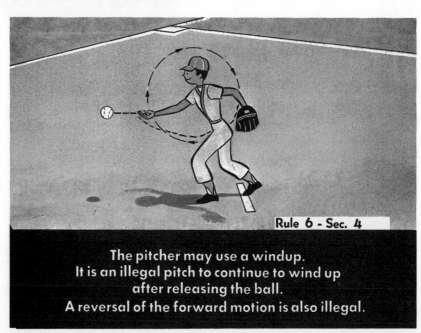

Rule 6 - Sec. 4

The pitcher may use a windup.
It is an illegal pitch to continue to wind up
after releasing the ball.
A reversal of the forward motion is also illegal.

Rule 6 - Sec. 3

The ball is delivered with an underhand motion.

Rule 6 - Sec. 2

The step *must* be taken simultaneously with the delivery of the ball. In Slow Pitch the ball must arch at least 3 feet after leaving the pitcher's hand and before it passes across home plate. The maximum height of a pitch in Slow Pitch shall not exceed 12 feet from the ground.

Ball is dead.

An illegal pitch is an unfairly delivered ball.

Rule 6 - Sec. 2

In Fast Pitch an illegal pitch results in a ball for the batter and a base for the runner. In Slow Pitch runners are not awarded a base.

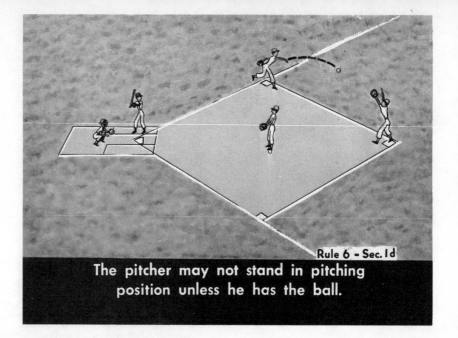

Rule 6 - Sec. 1d

The pitcher may not stand in pitching position unless he has the ball.

Ball is dead.

An illegal pitch

Rule 6 - Sec. 5

The ball may not be deliberately rolled along the ground.
This rule does not apply in Slow Pitch.

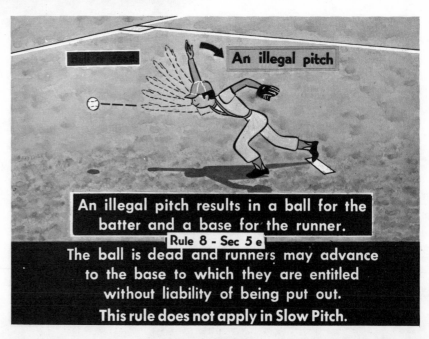

An illegal pitch

An illegal pitch results in a ball for the batter and a base for the runner.

Rule 8 - Sec 5 e

The ball is dead and runners may advance to the base to which they are entitled without liability of being put out.
This rule does not apply in Slow Pitch.

Rule 6—Sec. 6

No foreign substance may be put on the ball.

An illegal pitch   **Rule 6—Sec. 6**

He may not deface the ball in any way before pitching. (Could be ejected from game.)

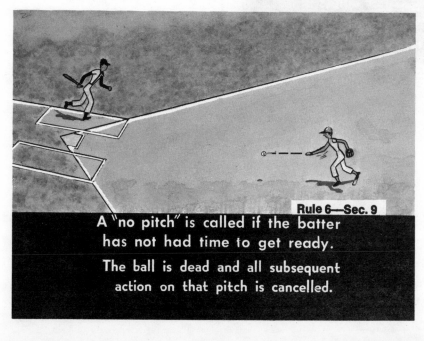

Rule 6—Sec. 9

A "no pitch" is called if the batter has not had time to get ready.

The ball is dead and all subsequent action on that pitch is cancelled.

A "NO PITCH" CANCELS ANY ACTION RESULTING FROM THAT PITCH.

Ball is dead.

Rule 6—Sec. 9

A "no pitch" is called if the pitcher pitches during suspension of play.

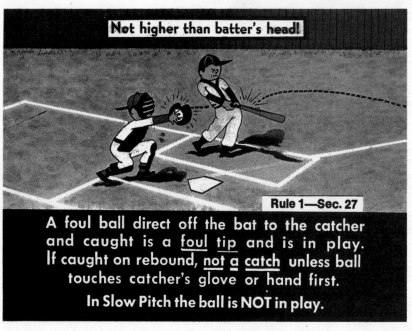

Not higher than batter's head!

Rule 1—Sec. 27

A foul ball direct off the bat to the catcher and caught is a foul tip and is in play. If caught on rebound, not a catch unless ball touches catcher's glove or hand first.

In Slow Pitch the ball is NOT in play.

A legal advance

Rule 8—Sec. 9i

A runner who has started to advance cannot be stopped by the pitcher stepping on the plate with the ball in his possession.

This rule does not apply in Slow Pitch.

When the ball is dead

Rule 1—Sec. 4

The pitcher puts the ball in play to restart the game— *after* umpire calls "Play ball."

OFFICIAL RULES FOR PITCHING

(Rule 6)

Fast Pitch

Sec. 1. THE PITCHER SHALL TAKE A POSITION WITH BOTH FEET FIRMLY ON THE GROUND AND IN CONTACT WITH, BUT NOT OFF THE SIDE OF, THE PITCHER'S PLATE.
a. Preliminary to pitching, the pitcher must come to a full and complete stop facing the batter with the shoulders in line with first and third base, and with the ball held in both hands in front of the body.
b. This position must be maintained at least 2 seconds and not more than 20 seconds before starting the delivery.
c. The pitcher shall not be considered in pitching position unless the catcher is in position to receive the pitch.
d. The pitcher may not take the pitching position on or near the pitcher's plate without having the ball in his possession.

Sec. 2. THE PITCH starts when one hand is taken off the ball or the pitcher makes any motion that is part of his wind-up. In the act of delivering the ball, the pitcher shall not take more than one step which must be forward, toward the batter, and simultaneous with the delivery of the ball to the batter. The pivot foot must remain in contact with the pitcher's plate until the other foot with which the pitcher steps toward home plate has touched the ground.
NOTE: It is not a step if the pitcher slides his foot across the pitcher's plate, provided contact is maintained with the pitcher's plate.

Sec. 3. A LEGAL DELIVERY SHALL BE A BALL WHICH IS DELIVERED TO THE BATTER WITH AN UNDERHAND MOTION.
a. The release of the ball and the follow through of the hand and wrist must be forward past the straight line of the body.
b. The hand shall be below the hip and the wrist not farther from the body than the elbow.
c. The pitch is completed with a step toward the batter.
d. The catcher must be within the outside lines of the catcher's box when the pitch is released.
e. The catcher shall return the ball directly to the pitcher after each pitch except after a strike out, or putout made by the catcher. The pitcher has 20 seconds to release the next pitch.
EXCEPTION — Sec. 3e: Does not apply with runners on base.
EFFECT — Sec. 3e: An additional "ball" is awarded to the batter.

Sec. 4. THE PITCHER MAY USE ANY WIND-UP DESIRED PROVIDING:
a. He does not make any motion to pitch without immediately delivering the ball to the batter.
b. He does not use a rocker action in which, after having the ball in both hands in pitching position, he removes one hand from the ball, takes a backward and forward swing and returns the ball to both hands in front of the body.
c. He does not use a wind-up in which there is a stop or reversal of the forward motion.
d. He does not make more than one revolution of the arm in the windmill pitch. A pitcher may drop his arm to the side and to the rear before starting the windmill motion.
e. He does not continue to wind-up after taking the forward step which is simultaneous with the release of the ball.

Sec. 5. THE PITCHER SHALL NOT DELIBERATELY DROP, ROLL OR BOUNCE THE BALL WHILE IN PITCHING POSITION IN ORDER TO PREVENT THE BATTER FROM STRIKING IT.

Sec. 6. THE PITCHER SHALL NOT AT ANY TIME DURING THE GAME BE ALLOWED TO USE TAPE OR OTHER SUBSTANCE UPON THE BALL, THE PITCHING HAND OR FINGERS. Under the supervision and control of the umpire powdered resin may be used to dry the hands. The pitcher shall not wear a sweatband, bracelet, or similar type item on the wrist or forearm of the pitching arm.
EFFECT—Sec. 1-6: Any infraction of Sections 1 thru 6 is an illegal pitch with the exception of Section 3e which is covered separately. The ball is dead. A ball is called on the batter. Baserunners are entitled to advance one base without liability to be put out. Exception—if the pitcher completes the delivery of the ball to the batter and the batter hits the ball and reaches first base safely and all baserunners advance at least one base then the play stands and the illegal pitch is nullified. A delayed dead ball will be signified by the umpire by extending his left arm horizontally.
NOTE: An illegal pitch shall be called immediately when it becomes illegal. If called by the plate umpire, it shall be called in a voice so that the catcher and the batter will hear it. The plate umpire will also give the delayed dead ball signal. If called by the base umpire, it shall be called so that the nearest fielder shall hear it. The base umpire shall also give the delayed dead ball signal. Failure of players to hear the call shall not void the call.

Sec. 7. AT THE BEGINNING OF EACH HALF INNING OR WHEN A PITCHER RELIEVES ANOTHER, NO MORE THAN 1 MINUTE MAY BE USED TO DELIVER NO MORE THAN 5 PITCHES TO THE CATCHER OR OTHER TEAMMATE. Play shall be suspended during this time. For excessive warm-up pitches a pitcher shall be penalized by awarding a ball to the batter for each pitch in excess of 5.

Sec. 8. THE PITCHER SHALL NOT THROW TO A BASE WHILE HIS FOOT IS IN CONTACT WITH THE PITCHER'S PLATE AFTER HE HAS TAKEN THE PITCHING POSITION.
EFFECT — Sec. 8: Illegal pitch, the ball is dead, a ball is called on the batter and all runners advance one base. If the throw from the pitcher's plate is during an appeal play, the appeal is cancelled.
NOTE: The pitcher can remove himself from the pitching position by stepping backwards off the pitcher's plate. Stepping forward or sideways constitutes an illegal pitch.

Sec. 9. NO PITCH SHALL BE DECLARED WHEN:
a. The pitcher pitches during the suspension of play.
b. The pitcher attempts a quick return of the ball before the batter has taken position or is off balance as a result of a previous pitch.
c. The runner is called out for leaving the base too soon.
d. The pitcher pitches before a baserunner has retouched his base after a foul ball has been declared and the ball is dead.
EFFECT — SEC. 9 a-d: The ball is dead and all subsequent action on that pitch is cancelled.
e. NO PLAYER, MANAGER OR COACH SHALL CALL "TIME" OR EMPLOY ANY OTHER WORD OR PHRASE OR COMMIT ANY ACT WHILE THE BALL IS ALIVE AND IN PLAY FOR THE OBVIOUS PURPOSE OF TRYING TO MAKE THE PITCHER COMMIT AN ILLEGAL PITCH.
EFFECT. — Sec. 9e: No pitch shall be declared and a warning issued to the offending team. A repeat of this type act by the team warned shall result in the offender being removed from the game.

Sec. 10. THERE SHALL BE ONLY ONE CHARGED CONFERENCE BETWEEN THE MANAGER OR OTHER TEAM REPRESENTATIVE FROM THE DUGOUT WITH EACH AND EVERY PITCHER IN AN INNING. The second charged conference shall result in the removal of the pitcher from the pitching position for the remainder of the game.

Sec. 11. IF THE BALL SLIPS FROM THE PITCHER'S HAND DURING HIS WINDUP OR DURING THE BACKSWING, THE BALL WILL BE IN PLAY AND THE RUNNERS MAY ADVANCE AT THEIR OWN RISK.

Slow Pitch

Sec. 1. THE PITCHER SHALL TAKE A POSITION WITH ONE OR BOTH FEET FIRMLY ON THE GROUND AND IN CONTACT WITH, BUT NOT OFF THE SIDE OF THE PITCHER'S PLATE. At the time of delivery, both the pivot and the non-pivot foot must be within the length (24 inches (600 mm)) of the pitcher's plate.

a. Preliminary to pitching, the pitcher must come to a full and complete stop facing the batter with the shoulders in line with first and third base, and with the ball held in one or both hands in front of the body.

b. This position must be maintained at least 2 seconds and not more than 20 seconds before starting the delivery.

c. The pitcher shall not be considered in pitching position unless the catcher is in position to receive the pitch.

Sec. 2. THE PITCH starts when the pitcher makes any motion that is part of his wind-up after the required pause. Prior to the required pause, any wind-up may be used. THE PIVOT FOOT MUST REMAIN IN CONTACT WITH THE PITCHER'S PLATE UNTIL THE PITCHED BALL LEAVES THE HAND. It is not necessary to step, but if a step is taken, it must be forward, toward the batter, within the length (24 inches (600 mm)) of the pitcher's plate, and simultaneous with the release of the ball.

Sec. 3. A LEGAL DELIVERY SHALL BE A BALL WHICH IS DELIVERED TO THE BATTER WITH AN UNDERHAND MOTION.

a. The pitch shall be released at a moderate speed. The speed is left entirely up to the umpire. The umpire shall warn the pitcher who delivers a pitch with excessive speed. If the pitcher repeats such an act after being warned, he shall be removed from the pitcher's position for the remainder of the game.

b. The hand shall be below the hip.

c. The ball must be delivered with a perceptible arch of at least 3 feet (0.99 m) from the time it leaves the pitcher's hand until it reaches home plate. The pitched ball shall not reach a height of more than 12 feet (3.96 m) at its highest point above the ground.

d. The catcher must be within the outside lines of the catcher's box until the pitched ball is batted, or reaches home plate.

e. The catcher shall return the ball directly to the pitcher after each pitch except after a strike out, or putout made by the catcher. The pitcher has 20 seconds to release the next pitch.

EFFECT — Sec. 3e: An additional "ball" is awarded to the batter.

Sec. 4. THE PITCHER MAY USE ANY WIND-UP DESIRED PROVIDING:

a. He does not make any motion to pitch without immediately delivering the ball to the batter.

b. His wind-up is a continuous motion.

c. He does not use a wind-up in which there is a stop or reversal of the forward motion.

d. He delivers the ball toward home plate on the first forward swing of the pitching arm past the hip.

e. He does not continue to wind-up after he releases the ball.

Sec. 5. THE PITCHER SHALL NOT DELIBERATELY DROP, ROLL OR BOUNCE THE BALL WHILE IN THE PITCHING POSITION IN ORDER TO PREVENT THE BATTER FROM STRIKING IT.

Sec. 6. THE PITCHER SHALL NOT AT ANY TIME DURING THE GAME BE ALLOWED TO USE TAPE OR OTHER SUBSTANCE UPON THE BALL, THE PITCHING HAND OR FINGERS. Under the supervision and control of the umpire powdered resin may be used to dry the hands. The pitcher shall not wear a sweatband, bracelet or similar type item on the wrist or forearm of the pitching arm.

Sec. 7. AT THE BEGINNING OF EACH HALF INNING OR WHEN A PITCHER RELIEVES ANOTHER, NO MORE THAN 1 MINUTE MAY BE USED TO DELIVER NO MORE THAN 5 PITCHES TO THE CATCHER OR OTHER TEAMMATE. Play shall be suspended during this time. For excessive warm-up pitches, a pitcher shall be penalized by awarding a ball to the batter for each pitch in excess of 5.

Sec. 8. THE PITCHER SHALL NOT THROW TO A BASE WHILE HIS FOOT IS IN CONTACT WITH THE PITCHER'S PLATE AFTER HE HAS TAKEN THE PITCHING POSITION.

NOTE: The pitcher can remove himself from the pitching position by stepping backwards off the pitcher's plate. Stepping forward or sideways constitutes an illegal pitch.

EFFECT — Sec. 1-8: Any infraction of Sections 1 thru 8 is an illegal pitch. The ball is dead. A ball shall be called on the batter. Baserunners do not advance.

EXCEPTION—If a batter strikes at any illegal pitch it shall be a strike and there shall be no penalty for such an illegal pitch. The ball shall remain in play if hit by the batter. If an illegal pitch is called during an appeal play, the appeal is cancelled.

NOTE: An illegal pitch shall be called immediately when it becomes illegal. If called by the plate umpire, it shall be called in a voice so that the catcher and the batter will hear it. The plate umpire will also give the delayed dead ball signal. If called by the base umpire, it shall be called so that the nearest fielder shall hear it. The base umpire shall also give the delayed dead ball signal. Failure of players to hear the call shall not void the call.

Sec. 9. NO PITCH SHALL BE DECLARED WHEN:

a. The pitcher pitches during the suspension of play.

b. **The pitcher attempts a quick return of the ball before the batter has taken his position or is off balance as a result of a previous pitch.**

c. The runner is called out for leaving the base too soon.

d. The pitcher pitches before the baserunner has retouched his base after a foul ball has been declared and the ball is dead.

e. THE BALL SLIPS FROM THE PITCHER'S HAND DURING HIS WIND-UP OR DURING THE BACKSWING.

EFFECT—Sec. 9a-e: The ball is dead and all subsequent action on that pitch is cancelled.

f. NO PLAYER, MANAGER OR COACH SHALL CALL "TIME" OR EMPLOY ANY OTHER WORD OR PHRASE OR COMMIT ANY ACT WHILE THE BALL IS ALIVE AND IN PLAY FOR THE OBVIOUS PURPOSE OF TRYING TO MAKE THE PITCHER COMMIT AN ILLEGAL PITCH.

EFFECT—Sec. 9f: No pitch shall be declared and a warning issued to the offending team. A repeat of this type act by the team warned shall result in the offender being removed from the game.

Sec. 10. THERE SHALL BE ONLY ONE CHARGED CONFERENCE BETWEEN THE MANAGER, OR OTHER TEAM REPRESENTATIVE FROM THE DUGOUT WITH EACH AND EVERY PITCHER IN AN INNING. The second charged conference shall result in the removal of the pitcher from the pitching position for the remainder of the game.

THE BATTER

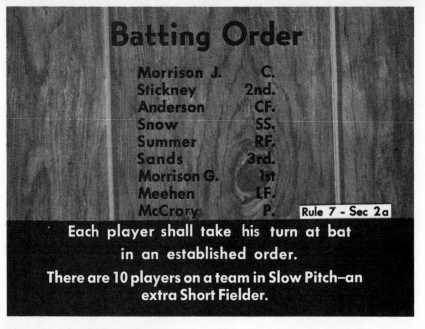

Batting Order

Morrison J.	C.
Stickney	2nd.
Anderson	CF.
Snow	SS.
Summer	RF.
Sands	3rd.
Morrison G.	1st
Meehen	LF.
McCrory	P.

Rule 7 - Sec 2a

Each player shall take his turn at bat in an established order.

There are 10 players on a team in Slow Pitch—an extra Short Fielder.

Rule 7 - Sec 1

The batter must stand with both feet within the batter's box.

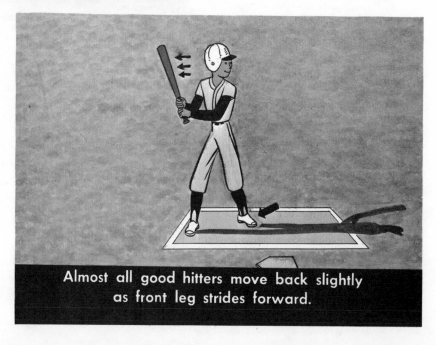

Almost all good hitters move back slightly as front leg strides forward.

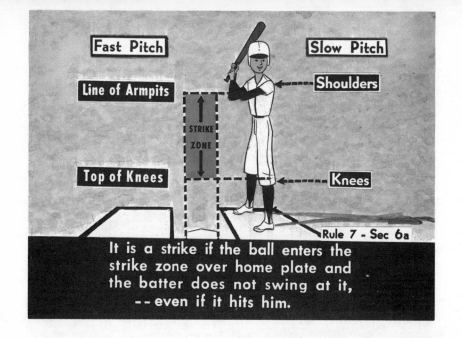

Fast Pitch

Slow Pitch

Line of Armpits

Shoulders

STRIKE ZONE

Top of Knees

Knees

Rule 7 - Sec 6a

It is a strike if the ball enters the strike zone over home plate and the batter does not swing at it, -- even if it hits him.

Rule 7 - Sec 1c

The batter may not use an illegal bat.

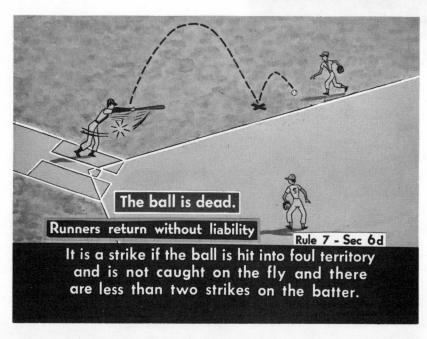

The ball is dead.

Runners return without liability

Rule 7 - Sec 6d

It is a strike if the ball is hit into foul territory and is not caught on the fly and there are less than two strikes on the batter.

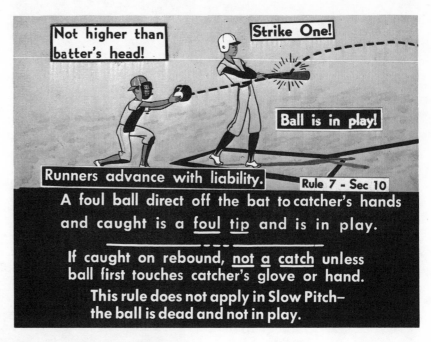

Not higher than batter's head!

Strike One!

Ball is in play!

Runners advance with liability.

Rule 7 - Sec 10

A foul ball direct off the bat to catcher's hands and caught is a _foul_ _tip_ and is in play.

If caught on rebound, <u>not a catch</u> unless ball first touches catcher's glove or hand.

This rule does not apply in Slow Pitch—
the ball is dead and not in play.

STRIKE ONE!

The ball remains in play.

Rule 7 - Sec 6b

It is a strike if the ball is swung at
and missed.
In Slow Pitch the ball is dead. Rule 9, Sec. x.

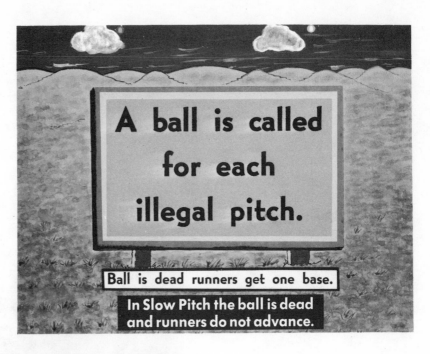

A ball is called for each illegal pitch.

Ball is dead runners get one base.

In Slow Pitch the ball is dead and runners do not advance.

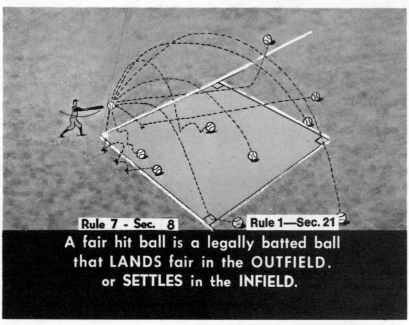

Rule 7 - Sec. 8   Rule 1—Sec. 21

A fair hit ball is a legally batted ball that LANDS fair in the OUTFIELD. or SETTLES in the INFIELD.

The batter becomes a baserunner

Go to First!

Ball remains in play.

Advance with liability

Rule 8 - Sec 2f

It is a fair ball if it strikes a player on fair
territory - after a fielder has had a chance
to make a play.

Ball is in play

Rule 8 - Sec 2f

Rule 9—Sec. 2f

It is a fair ball if it strikes a player or umpire
in fair territory after a fielder has had
a chance to make a play.

AN INFIELD FLY

An infield fly is a fair fly by the batter (which can reasonably be handled by an infielder) when there are less than two outs and runners on first and second, or first, second and third.

The umpire shall declare "Infield fly"

The batter is out and runners may advance at their own risk. Rule 1—Sec. 35

This does not include a line drive or an attempted bunt.

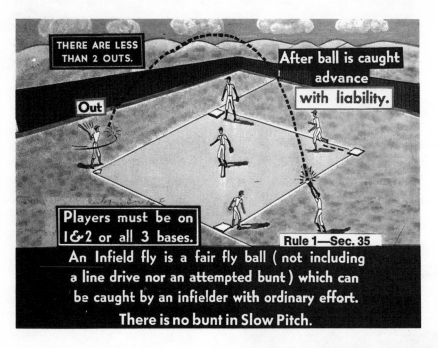

THERE ARE LESS THAN 2 OUTS.

Out

After ball is caught advance with liability.

Players must be on 1&2 or all 3 bases.

Rule 1—Sec. 35

An Infield fly is a fair fly ball (not including a line drive nor an attempted bunt) which can be caught by an infielder with ordinary effort.

There is no bunt in Slow Pitch.

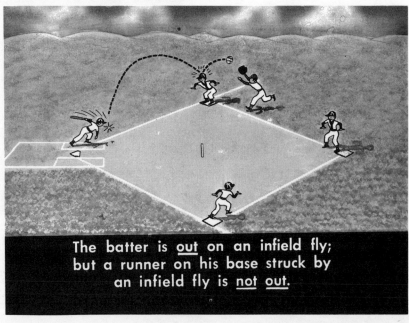

The batter is <u>out</u> on an infield fly; but a runner on his base struck by an infield fly is <u>not out</u>.

"A good guide" to determine if infield fly: Could fielder be facing toward batter when making catch? Here NOT an infield fly.

What happens if a batter bats out of turn?

Rule 7 - Sec 2

It is an appeal play if a player bats out of turn.

incorrect batter

Rule 7—Sec. 2c(1)

#2 takes over with the 2 strikes and 2 balls. Bases run and scores made stand.

The proper batter #2 comes to bat and assumes the ball and strike count of the improper batter # 3.

YOU'RE OUT

Go back!

Go back to bat!

Rule 7—Sec. 2c(2)

If an appeal is made after #3 has completed his time at bat, #2 is out. Bases run and scores made do not count.

Not out

Too late to appeal now!

Run counts

Rule 7—Sec. 2c(3)

If the error is not discovered and the pitcher pitches to #4 the game continues. All bases run and scores made stand.

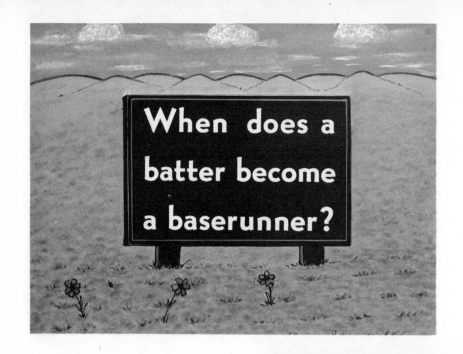

When does a
batter become
a baserunner?

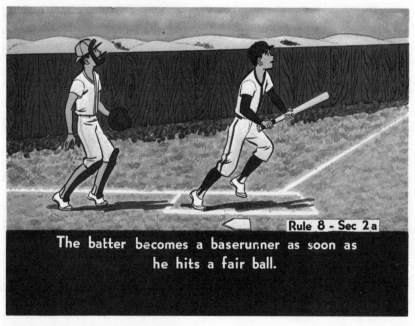

Rule 8 - Sec 2a

The batter becomes a baserunner as soon as
he hits a fair ball.

Ball is dead

The batter is awarded 1st base if the catcher
or any other fielder, interferes with him.

Rule 8 - Sec 2 e

Ball is in play

Rule 8 - Sec 2 b

- if less than 2 out and 1st base is not occupied.

A batter may run when he has three strikes
- if the catcher fails to catch the ball.
3rd Strike Rule

The Third Strike Rule does not apply in Slow Pitch.

Third Strike Rule

When the catcher fails to catch the 3rd strike
before the ball touches the ground when
there are less than two outs and 1st base
is unoccupied, or anytime there are 2 outs.
This is called the 3rd Strike Rule
The Third Strike Rule does not apply in Slow Pitch.

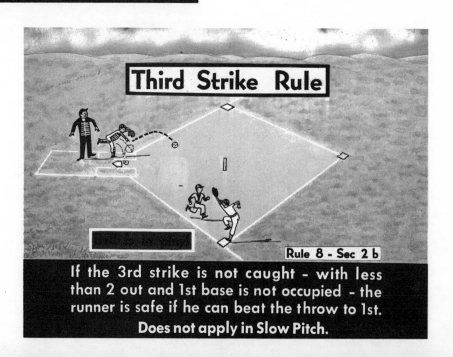

Third Strike Rule

Rule 8 - Sec 2 b

If the 3rd strike is not caught - with less
than 2 out and 1st base is not occupied - the
runner is safe if he can beat the throw to 1st.
Does not apply in Slow Pitch.

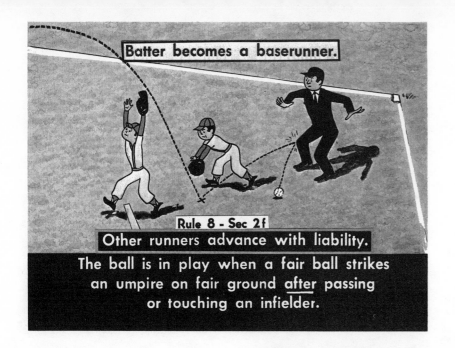

Batter becomes a baserunner.

Rule 8 - Sec 2f

Other runners advance with liability.

The ball is in play when a fair ball strikes an umpire on fair ground <u>after</u> passing or touching an infielder.

GO TO 3RD!

Batter becomes a baserunner

Rule 8 - Sec. 2f

The <u>ball</u> <u>is</u> <u>in</u> <u>play</u> when a fair ball strikes a runner on fair ground <u>after</u> passing or touching an infielder.

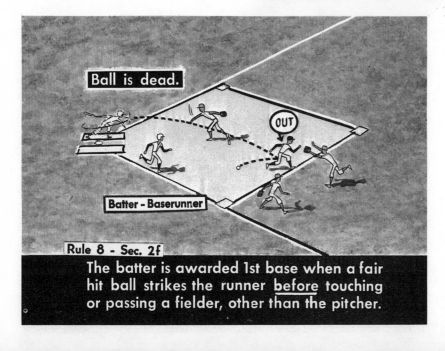

Ball is dead.

OUT

Batter - Baserunner

Rule 8 - Sec. 2f

The batter is awarded 1st base when a fair hit ball strikes the runner <u>before</u> touching or passing a fielder, other than the pitcher.

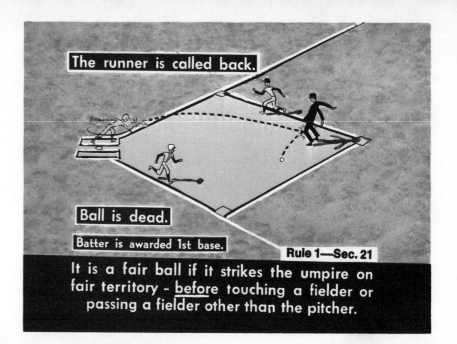

The runner is called back.

Ball is dead.

Batter is awarded 1st base.

Rule 1—Sec. 21

It is a fair ball if it strikes the umpire on fair territory - <u>before</u> touching a fielder or passing a fielder other than the pitcher.

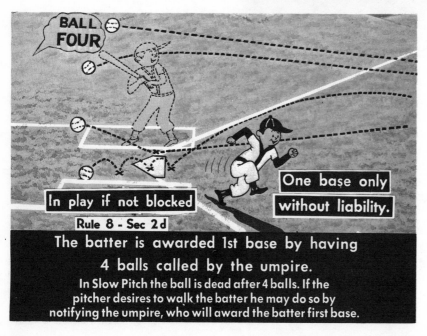

BALL FOUR

In play if not blocked

Rule 8 - Sec 2d

One base only without liability.

The batter is awarded 1st base by having 4 balls called by the umpire.

In Slow Pitch the ball is dead after 4 balls. If the pitcher desires to walk the batter he may do so by notifying the umpire, who will award the batter first base.

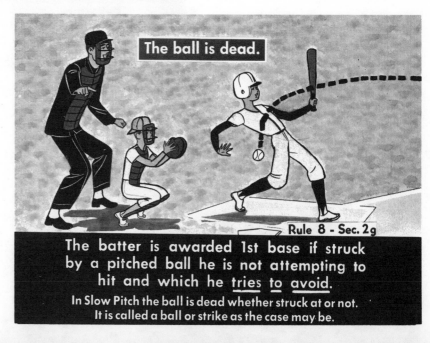

The ball is dead.

Rule 8 - Sec. 2g

The batter is awarded 1st base if struck by a pitched ball he is not attempting to hit and which he <u>tries</u> <u>to</u> <u>avoid</u>.

In Slow Pitch the ball is dead whether struck at or not. It is called a ball or strike as the case may be.

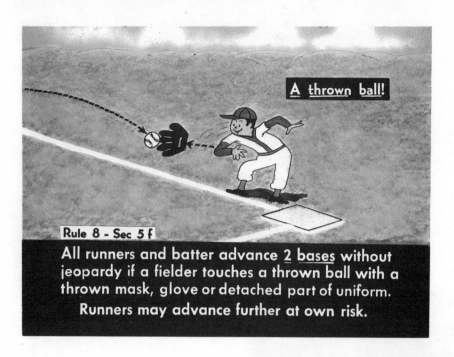

A thrown ball!

Rule 8 - Sec 5 f

All runners and batter advance <u>2 bases</u> without jeopardy if a fielder touches a thrown ball with a thrown mask, glove or detached part of uniform.

Runners may advance further at own risk.

Rule 8 - Sec 5 f

All runners and batter are entitled to advance home without jeopardy when ball is prevented from going over the fence by a fielder striking it with a thrown glove, apparel or equipment.

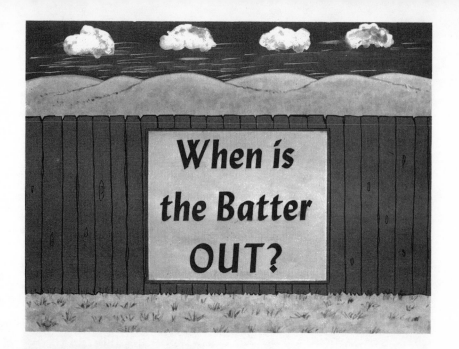

When is the Batter OUT?

Runners advance with liability.

Out

1 MIN.

Rule 7—Sec. 1e

The batter is out if he fails to take his position within 1 minute after the umpire has called for the batter.

Some of the ways a batter can be put out.

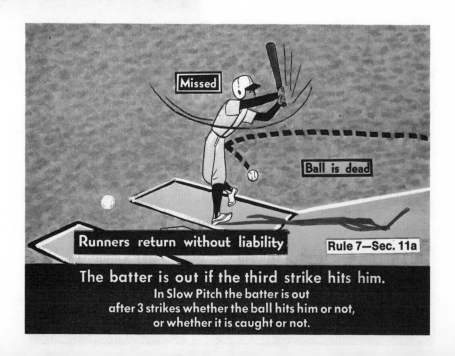

Missed

Ball is dead

Runners return without liability

Rule 7—Sec. 11a

The batter is out if the third strike hits him.
In Slow Pitch the batter is out
after 3 strikes whether the ball hits him or not,
or whether it is caught or not.

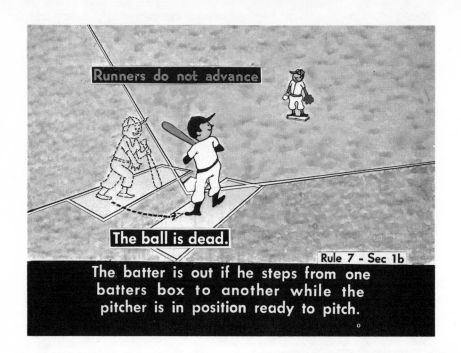

Runners do not advance

The ball is dead.

Rule 7 - Sec 1b

The batter is out if he steps from one batters box to another while the pitcher is in position ready to pitch.

Runners may not advance!

The batter is <u>out</u> if his fair hit ball bounces up and hits him outside the batter's box <u>before</u> touching a fielder.

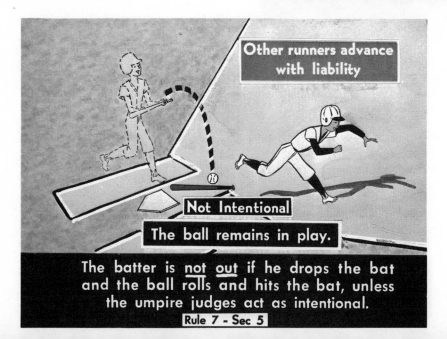

Other runners advance with liability

Not Intentional

The ball remains in play.

The batter is <u>not</u> <u>out</u> if he drops the bat and the ball rolls and hits the bat, unless the umpire judges act as intentional.

Rule 7 - Sec 5

Runners do not advance

Rule 7—Sec. 11i

**The batter is out if he bunts
the third strike foul.**

There is no bunt in Slow Pitch. The batter is
always out if he bunts or chops the ball downward.

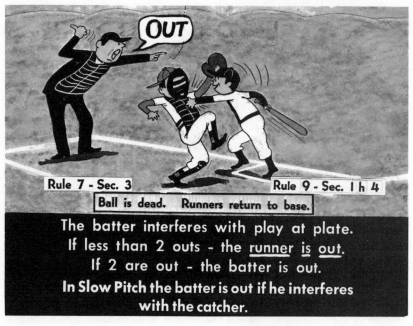

OUT

Rule 7 - Sec. 3

Rule 9 - Sec. 1 h 4

Ball is dead.   Runners return to base.

**The batter interferes with play at plate.
If less than 2 outs - the <u>runner</u> <u>is</u> <u>out</u>.
If 2 are out - the batter is out.**

**In Slow Pitch the batter is out if he interferes
with the catcher.**

Could occur at any base

3 Ft.

The ball is in play.

Rule 8—Sec. 8a

**The runner is out if he runs <u>outside</u> the
base path to avoid being tagged.**

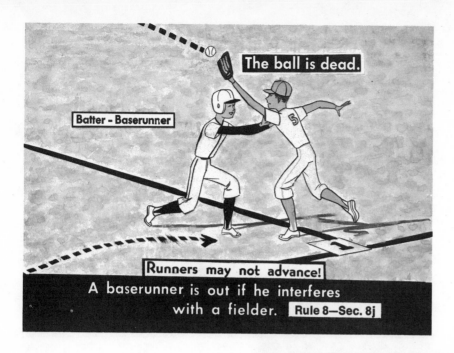

The ball is dead.

Batter - Baserunner

Runners may not advance!

A baserunner is out if he interferes with a fielder. **Rule 8—Sec. 8j**

Batter - Baserunner

OUT

Rule 8—Sec. 7c

The batter is <u>out</u> <u>if</u> <u>touched</u> before he reaches 1st base on a fair hit ball, or on a 3rd strike which is not caught.

There is no 3rd Strike Rule in Slow Pitch.

A Force-Out

Batter - Baserunner

Rule 1—Sec. 25
Rule 8—Sec. 8c

The runner is <u>out</u> when the base to which he is advancing on a Force Play is tagged.

THERE ARE LESS THAN 2 OUTS.

or anytime there are 2 outs.

not occupied.

Rule 8 - Sec 2 b

However, the batter is <u>not out</u> if the catcher drops the 3rd strike — and first base is not occupied with a baserunner.

This rule does not apply in Slow Pitch.

Ball is in play

Rule 8—Sec. 2b

The batter is out, if on a dropped third strike, he is tagged or <u>thrown out</u> before reaching first base.

This rule does not apply in Slow Pitch.

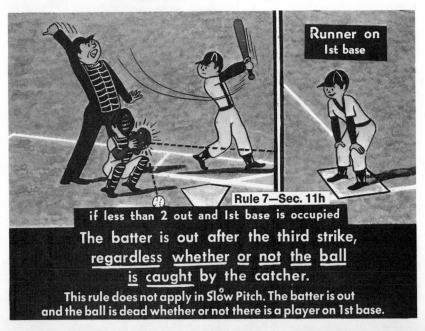

Runner on 1st base

Rule 7—Sec. 11h

if less than 2 out and 1st base is occupied

The batter is out after the third strike, regardless <u>whether</u> or <u>not the ball</u> <u>is caught</u> by the catcher.

This rule does not apply in Slow Pitch. The batter is out and the ball is dead whether or not there is a player on 1st base.

Rule 7—Sec. 11c

The batter is <u>out</u> if he hits a fair fly ball which is caught by a fielder before it touches the ground.

Out

Rule 7—Sec. 11c

The <u>batter</u> <u>is</u> <u>out</u> if he hits a foul fly ball which is caught by a fielder before it touches the ground.

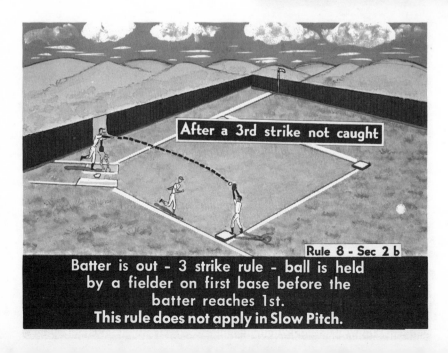

After a 3rd strike not caught

Rule 8 - Sec 2 b

Batter is out - 3 strike rule - ball is held by a fielder on first base before the batter reaches 1st.
This rule does not apply in Slow Pitch.

The batter is out on an infield fly; but a runner on his base struck by an infield fly is not out.

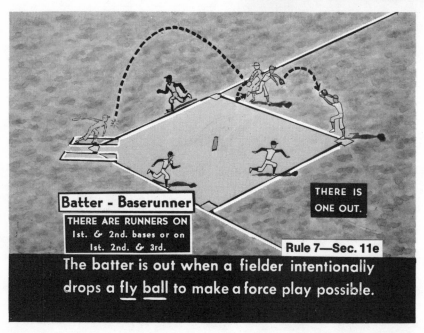

Batter - Baserunner

THERE ARE RUNNERS ON 1st. & 2nd. bases or on 1st. 2nd. & 3rd.

THERE IS ONE OUT.

Rule 7—Sec. 11e

The batter is out when a fielder intentionally drops a fly ball to make a force play possible.

THERE IS ONE OUT.

Rule 7—Sec. 11e

A batter is out when a fielder intentionally drops a line drive in order to make a force play possible.

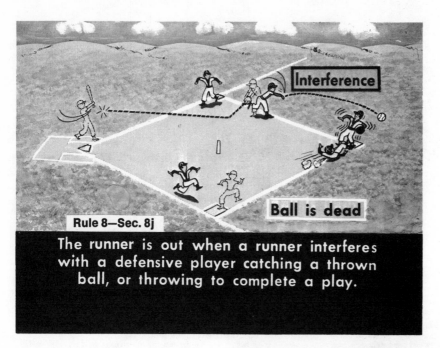

Interference

Ball is dead

Rule 8—Sec. 8j

The runner is out when a runner interferes with a defensive player catching a thrown ball, or throwing to complete a play.

Interference

Rule 8—Sec. 8j

If this interference, in the judgment of the umpire, is an obvious attempt to prevent a double play, the immediate succeeding runner shall also be called out.

OFFICIAL RULES FOR BATTING

(Rule 7)

Sec. 1. THE BATTER SHALL TAKE HIS POSITION WITHIN THE LINES OF THE BATTER'S BOX.

a. The batter shall not have his entire foot touching the ground completely outside the lines of the batter's box or touching home plate when the ball is hit.

b. The batter shall not step directly across in front of the catcher to the other batter's box while the pitcher is in position ready to pitch.

c. The batter shall not hit the ball with an illegal bat.
   EFFECT—Sec. 1a-c: The ball is dead, the batter is out, baserunners may NOT advance.

d. The batter shall not enter the batter's box with an altered bat.
   EFFECT—Sec. 1d: The ball is dead, the batter is out and without warning, the batter is removed from further participation in the game, and baserunners may not advance.

e. The batter must take his position within 1 minute after the umpire has called "play ball."
   EFFECT—Sec. 1e: The ball is dead. The batter is out.

Sec. 2 EACH PLAYER OF THE SIDE AT BAT SHALL BECOME A BATTER IN THE ORDER IN WHICH HIS NAME APPEARS ON THE SCORE-SHEET.

a. The batting order of each team must be on the score sheet and must be delivered before the game by the manager or captain to the plate umpire. He shall submit it to the inspection of the manager or captain of the opposing team.
   EFFECT—2a: The umpire shall declare a forfeit.

b. The batting order delivered to the umpire must be followed throughout the game unless a player is substituted for another. When this occurs the substitute must take the place of the removed player in the batting order.

c. The first batter in each inning shall be the batter whose name follows that of the last player who completed a turn at bat in the preceeding inning.
   EFFECT—Sec. 2b-c: Batting out of order is an appeal play which may be made by the defensive team only and while the ball is dead.
   (1) If the error is discovered while the incorrect batter is at bat, correct batter may take his place, assume any balls and strikes, and any runs scored or bases run while the incorrect batter was at bat shall be legal.
   (2) If the error is discovered after the incorrect batter has completed his turn at bat and before there has been a pitch to another batter, the player who should have batted is out. Any advance or score made because of a ball batted by the improper batter or because of the improper batter's advance to first base on a hit, an error, a base on balls, or a hit batter shall be nullified. The next batter is the player whose name follows that of the player called out for failing to bat. If the batter declared out under these circumstances is the third out, the correct batter in the next inning shall be the player who would have come to bat had the players been put out by ordinary play.
   (3) If the error is discovered after the first pitch to the next batter, the turn at bat of the incorrect batter is legal, all runs scored and bases run are legal, and the next batter in order shall be the one whose name follows that of the incorrect batter. No one is called out for failure to bat. Players who have not batted and who have not been called out have lost their turn at bat until reached again in the regular order.
   (4) No baserunner shall be removed from the base he is occupying to bat in his proper place. He merely misses his turn at bat with no penalty. The batter following him in the batting order becomes the legal batter.

d. When the third out in an inning is made before the batter has completed his turn at bat, he shall be the first batter in the next inning, and the ball and strike count on him shall be cancelled.

Sec. 3 THE BATTER SHALL NOT HINDER THE CATCHER FROM FIELDING OR THROWING THE BALL BY STEPPING OUT OF THE BATTER'S BOX, OR INTENTIONALLY HINDER THE CATCHER WHILE STANDING WITHIN THE BATTER'S BOX.

EFFECT—Sec. 3: The ball is dead and baserunners must return to the last base that in the judgment of the umpire was touched at the time of the interference. The batter is out except:
(1) (FP ONLY) If a baserunner attempting to steal is put out, the batter is not also out.
(2) With less than two outs and a runner on third base and the batter interferes with a play being made at home plate, the batter is not out because the runner is out.

Sec. 4. MEMBERS OF THE TEAM AT BAT SHALL NOT INTERFERE WITH A PLAYER ATTEMPTING TO FIELD A FOUL FLY BALL.

EFFECT—Sec. 4: The ball is dead and the batter is out, and baserunners must return to the base legally held at the time of the pitch.

Sec. 5. THE BATTER SHALL NOT HIT A FAIR BALL WITH THE BAT A SECOND TIME IN FAIR TERRITORY.

NOTE: If the batter drops the bat and the ball rolls against the bat in fair territory and, in the umpire's judgment, there was no intention to interfere with the course of the ball, the batter is not out and the ball is alive and in play.
EFFECT—Sec. 5: The ball is dead, the batter is out, and baserunners may not advance.

Sec. 6. A STRIKE IS CALLED BY THE UMPIRE:

a. (FP ONLY) For each legally pitched ball entering the strike zone before touching the ground at which the batter does not swing.
   EFFECT—Sec. 6a: (FP) The ball is in play and the baserunners may advance with liability to be put out. The batter is out if:
   (1) The catcher does not drop the third strike.
   (2) First base is occupied with less than two out.
   (SP ONLY) For each legally pitched ball entering the strike zone before touching the ground and at which the batter does not swing. It is not a strike if the pitched ball touches home plate and is not swung at.
   EFFECT—Sec. 6a: (SP) The ball is dead.

b. (FP ONLY) For each legally pitched ball struck at and missed by the batter.
   EFFECT—Sec. 6b: (FP) The ball is in play and the baserunners may advance with liability to be put out. The batter is out if:
   (1) The catcher does not drop the third strike.
   (2) First base is occupied with less than two out.
   (SP ONLY) For each pitched ball struck at and missed by the batter.
   EFFECT—Sec. 6b: (SP) The ball is dead.

c. For each foul tip held by the catcher.
   EFFECT—Sec. 6c: (FP) The ball is in play and baserunners may advance with liability to be put out. The batter is out if it is the third strike.
   EFFECT—Sec. 6c: (SP) The batter is out if it is the third strike. The ball is dead on any strike.

d. For each foul ball not legally caught on the fly when the batter has less than two strikes.

e. For each pitched ball struck at and missed which touches any part of the batter.

f. When any part of the batter's person is hit with his own batted ball when he is in the batter's box and he has less than two strikes.

g. When a delivered ball by the pitcher hits the batter while the ball is in the strike zone.
   EFFECT—Sec. 6d-g: The ball is dead and baserunners must return to their bases without liability to be put out.

Sec. 7. A BALL IS CALLED BY THE UMPIRE:

a. For each pitched ball which does not enter the strike zone or touches the ground before reaching home plate or touches home plate and which is not struck at by the batter.
  EFFECT—Sec. 7a: (FP) The ball is in play and baserunners are entitled to advance with liability to be put out.
  EFFECT—Sec. 7a: (SP) The ball is dead. Baserunners may not advance.
b. For each illegally pitched ball.
  EFFECT—Sec. 7b: (FP) The ball is dead and baserunners are entitled to advance one base without liability to be put out.
  EFFECT—Sec. 7b: (SP) The ball is dead. Baserunners may not advance.
c. (SP ONLY) When a delivered ball by the pitcher hits the batsman outside of the strike zone.
d. When the catcher fails to return the ball directly to the pitcher as required in Rule 6, Section 6.
e. When the pitcher fails to pitch the ball within 20 seconds.
f. For each excessive warm-up pitch.
  EFFECT—Sec. 7c-f: The ball is dead. Baserunners may not advance.

Sec. 8. A FAIR BALL IS A LEGALLY BATTED BALL WHICH:

a. Settles or is touched on fair ground between home and first base or between home and third base.
b. Bounds past first or third base on or over fair ground.
c. Touches first, second, or third base.
d. While on or over fair ground touches the person or clothing of an umpire or player.
e. First falls on fair ground beyond first or third base. A fair fly must be judged according to the relative position of the ball and the foul line regardless of whether the fielder is on fair or foul ground at the time he touches the ball.
  EFFECT—Sec. 8a-e: The ball is in play and baserunners are entitled to advance any number of bases with liability to be put out. The batter becomes a baserunner unless the infield fly rule applies.
f. While on or over fair ground, lands behind a fence or into a stand a distance of more than 225 feet (74.25 m) (Male & Female Fast Pitch), 250 feet (82.5 m) (Female Slow Pitch) or 275 feet (90.75 m) (Male Slow Pitch) from home plate. This is considered a home run. If the distance is less than 225 feet (74.25 m) (Male & Female Fast Pitch), or 250 feet (82.5 m) (Female Slow Pitch), or 275 feet (90.75 m) (Male Slow Pitch) from home plate, it is a 2 base hit.
g. Hits a foul line pole on the fly. If the ball hits the pole above the fence level, it shall be a home run.

Sec. 9. A FOUL BALL IS A LEGALLY BATTED BALL WHICH:

a. Settles on foul ground between home and first base or between home and third base.
b. Bounds past first or third base on or over foul ground.
c. First touches on foul ground beyond first or third base.
d. While on or over foul ground touches the person or clothing of an umpire, or player, or is blocked.
  EFFECT—Sec. 9a-d: (1) The ball is dead unless it is a legally caught foul fly. If a foul fly is caught the batter is out. (2) A strike is called on the batter unless he already had two strikes. (3) Baserunners must return to their bases without liability to be put out unless a foul fly is caught. In this case, the baserunner may advance with liability to be put out after the ball has been touched.

Sec. 10. A FOUL TIP IS A BATTED BALL WHICH GOES DIRECTLY FROM THE BAT, NOT HIGHER THAN THE BATTER'S HEAD, TO THE CATCHER'S HANDS AND IS LEGALLY CAUGHT BY THE CATCHER.

NOTE: It is not a foul tip unless caught and any foul tip that is caught is a strike. In Fast Pitch, the ball is in play, in Slow Pitch, the ball is dead.
EFFECT—Sec. 10 (FP): A strike is called, the ball remains in play and baserunners may advance with liability to be put out.
EFFECT—Sec. 10 (SP): A strike is called, the ball is dead.

Sec. 11. THE BATTER IS OUT UNDER THE FOLLOWING CIRCUMSTANCES:

a. When the third strike is struck at and missed and touches any part of the batter's person.
b. When a batter appears in the batter's box with, or is discovered using an altered bat.
c. When a fly ball is legally caught.
d. Immediately when he hits an infield fly with baserunners on first and second or on first, second and third with less than two out. This is called the infield fly rule.
e. The batter is out if a fielder intentionally drops a fair fly ball (including a line drive) (FP or SP) or a bunt (FP ONLY) which can be caught by an infielder, with ordinary effort, with 1st, 1st & 2nd, 1st & 3rd, or 1st, 2nd and 3rd base occupied with less than 2 outs.
  NOTE: A trapped ball shall not be considered as having been intentionally dropped.
  EFFECT—Sec. 11e: The ball is dead, and baserunners must return to the last base touched at the time of the pitch.
f. The batter-runner is out if a preceding runner who is not yet out, and in the umpire's judgment, intentionally interferes with a fielder who is attempting to catch a thrown ball or to throw a ball in an attempt to complete the play. The runner shall also be called out and interference called.
g. (FP ONLY) When the third strike is caught by the catcher.
h. (FP ONLY) When he has 3 strikes if there are less than 2 outs and first base is occupied.
i. (FP ONLY) When he bunts foul after the second strike. If the ball is caught in the air, it remains alive and in play.
j. (SP ONLY) When a third strike is called.
k. (SP ONLY) When he bunts or chops the ball downward.

Sec. 12. THE BATTER IS NOT OUT IF A FIELDER MAKING A PLAY ON HIM USES AN ILLEGAL GLOVE. The manager of the offended team has the option of having the batter bat over and assuming the ball and strike count he had prior to the pitch he hit, or taking the result of the play.

Sec. 13. ON DECK BATTER.

a. The on deck batter is the offensive player whose name follows the name of the batter in the batting order.
b. The on deck batter shall take a position within the lines of the on deck circle.
c. The on deck batter may leave the on deck circle:
  (1) When he becomes the batter.
  (2) To direct baserunners advancing from third to home plate.
d. When the on deck batter interferes with the defensive player's opportunity to make a play on a runner, the runner closest to home plate at the time of the interference shall be declared out.
e. The provision of Rule 7, Section 4, shall apply to the on deck batter.

THE BASERUNNER

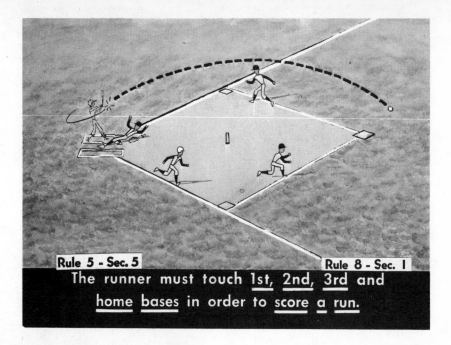

Rule 5 - Sec. 5   Rule 8 - Sec. I

The runner must touch <u>1st</u>, <u>2nd</u>, <u>3rd</u> and <u>home</u> <u>bases</u> in order to <u>score a run</u>.

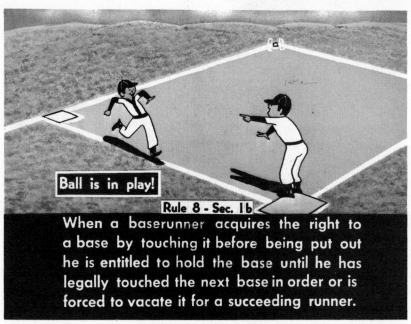

Ball is in play!

Rule 8 - Sec. Ib

When a baserunner acquires the right to a base by touching it before being put out he is entitled to hold the base until he has legally touched the next base in order or is forced to vacate it for a succeeding runner.

Advancing runner   Entitled to hold base

Rule 8 - Sec Ib   Rule 8 - Sec. Ie

If not a force play, the advancing runner is out, if tagged while two men occupy a base.

RUNS DO NOT SCORE

Rule 5—Sec. 7

Rule 8 - Sec 1 f

If a preceding runner is the 3rd
out on an appeal play.

3 OUTS

RUNS DO NOT SCORE

Rule 5 - Sec 6 b

If any other runner is put out
by a force out for 3rd out.

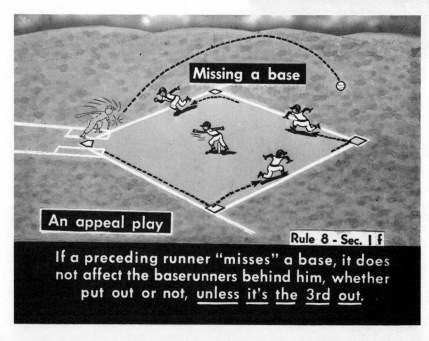

Missing a base

An appeal play

Rule 8 - Sec. 1 f

If a preceding runner "misses" a base, it does
not affect the baserunners behind him, whether
put out or not, unless it's the 3rd out.

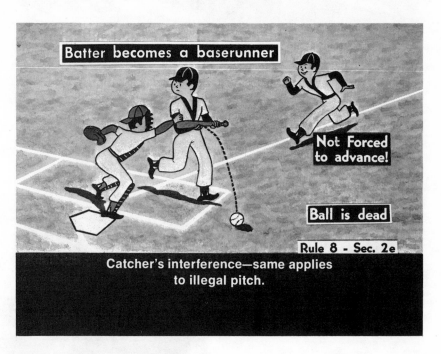

Catcher's interference—same applies
to illegal pitch.

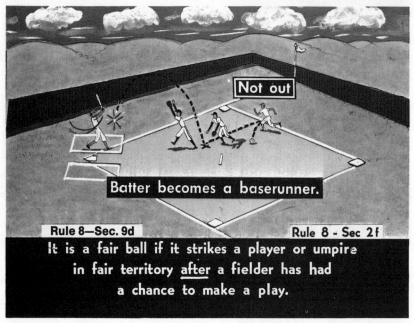

It is a fair ball if it strikes a player or umpire
in fair territory <u>after</u> a fielder has had
a chance to make a play.

The batter is awarded 1st base.

Go back

The ball is dead.

Rule 8 - Sec 2 e

Runner must return to last base touched
at the time of interference.

One base only

Go back!

Rule 8—Sec. 2f

Ball is dead

The batter is awarded 1st base when a fair
hit ball strikes the umpire <u>before</u> touching
or passing a fielder, other than the pitcher.

When may a baserunner try for another base?

with the liability of being put out

Runners advance with liability.

Ball is in play

Rule 8 - Sec. 3 b

A baserunner advances at his own risk when an overthrow is unobstructed in <u>fair</u> or <u>foul</u> territory.

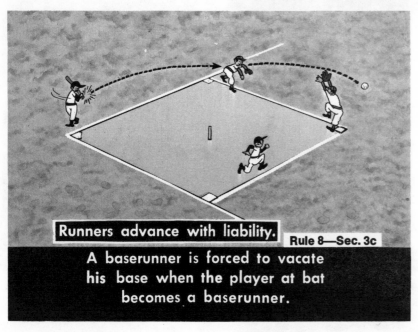

Runners advance with liability.

Rule 8—Sec. 3c

A baserunner is forced to vacate his base when the player at bat becomes a baserunner.

Runners may advance with liability

Rule 8 - Sec. 3 c

This situation is <u>not</u> a force play. First base is open for the batter.

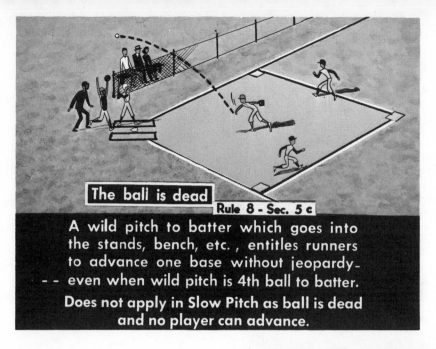

The ball is dead

Rule 8 - Sec. 5 c

A wild pitch to batter which goes into the stands, bench, etc., entitles runners to advance one base without jeopardy-- even when wild pitch is 4th ball to batter.

Does not apply in Slow Pitch as ball is dead and no player can advance.

When is the baserunner given the right to advance without risk?

Ball is dead

Rule 8 - Sec. 2g

If the pitch hits the batter and he has not swung at it, he is awarded 1st base.
Does not apply in Slow Pitch. Either a ball or strike is called as the case may be.
Ball is dead and no player advances.

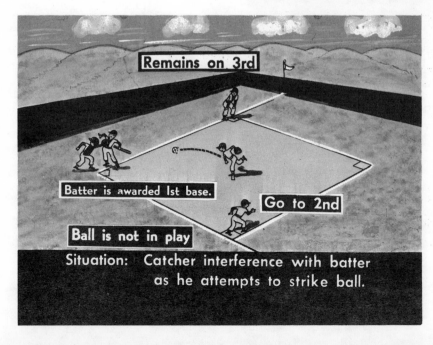

Remains on 3rd

Batter is awarded 1st base.

Go to 2nd

Ball is not in play

Situation: Catcher interference with batter as he attempts to strike ball.

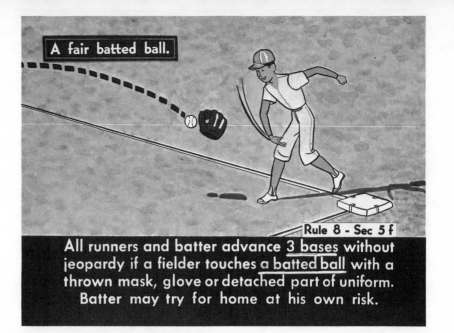

A fair batted ball.

Rule 8 - Sec 5 f

All runners and batter advance 3 bases without jeopardy if a fielder touches a batted ball with a thrown mask, glove or detached part of uniform. Batter may try for home at his own risk.

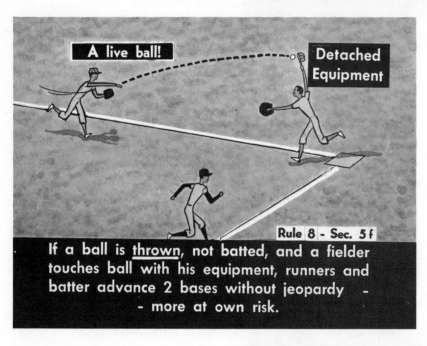

A live ball!

Detached Equipment

Rule 8 - Sec. 5 f

If a ball is thrown, not batted, and a fielder touches ball with his equipment, runners and batter advance 2 bases without jeopardy - - more at own risk.

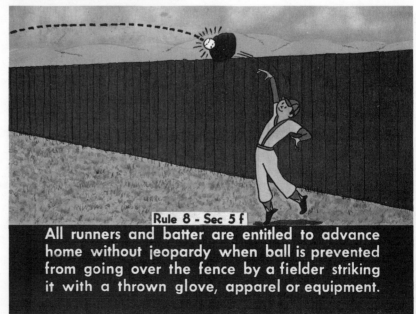

Rule 8 - Sec 5 f

All runners and batter are entitled to advance home without jeopardy when ball is prevented from going over the fence by a fielder striking it with a thrown glove, apparel or equipment.

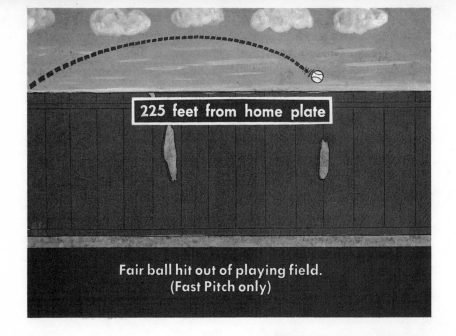

225 feet from home plate

Fair ball hit out of playing field.
(Fast Pitch only)

▲
In Slow Pitch
275 feet for Men
250 feet for Women ▶
is out of
the playing field.
▼

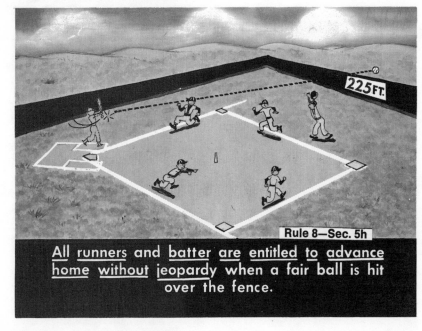

225 FT.

Rule 8—Sec. 5h

All runners and batter are entitled to advance
home without jeopardy when a fair ball is hit
over the fence.

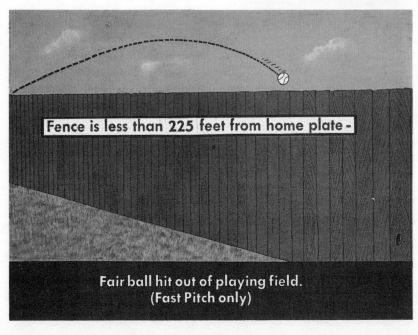

Fence is less than 225 feet from home plate -

Fair ball hit out of playing field.
(Fast Pitch only)

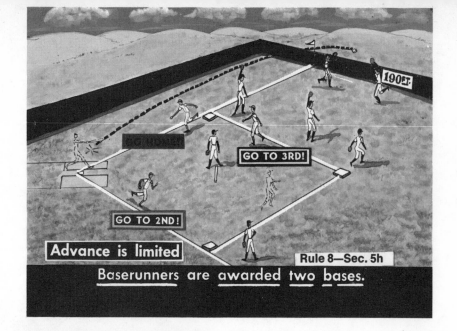

Advance is limited

GO TO 3RD!

GO TO 2ND!

190 FT.

Rule 8—Sec. 5h

Baserunners are awarded two bases.

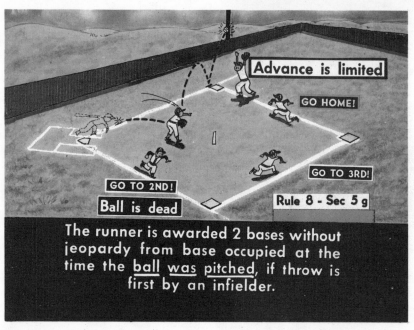

Advance is limited

GO HOME!

GO TO 3RD!

GO TO 2ND!

Ball is dead

Rule 8 - Sec 5 g

The runner is awarded 2 bases without jeopardy from base occupied at the time the ball was pitched, if throw is first by an infielder.

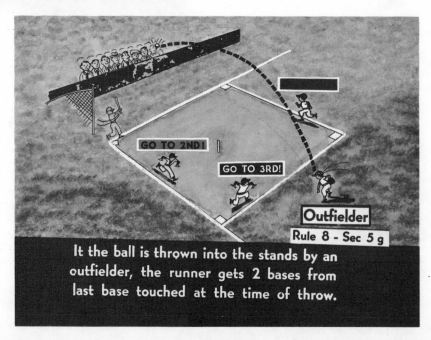

GO TO 2ND!

GO TO 3RD!

Outfielder

Rule 8 - Sec 5 g

It the ball is thrown into the stands by an outfielder, the runner gets 2 bases from last base touched at the time of throw.

A baserunner is forced to vacate
his base when the player at bat
becomes a baserunner.
In Slow Pitch the ball is dead.

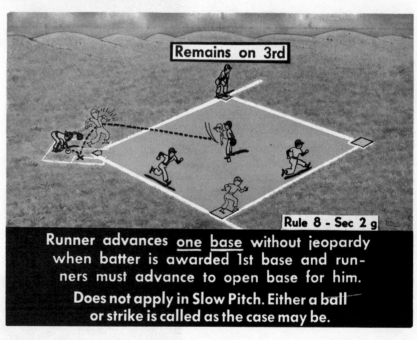

Runner advances **one base** without jeopardy
when batter is awarded 1st base and runners must advance to open base for him.

Does not apply in Slow Pitch. Either a ball
or strike is called as the case may be.

When must a baserunner return to base?

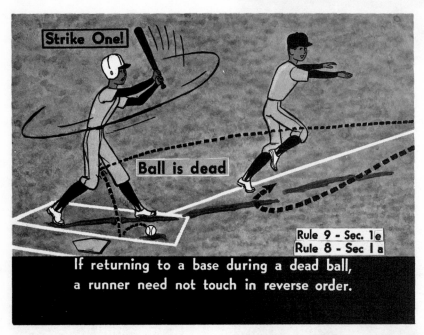

Strike One!

Ball is dead

Rule 9 - Sec. 1e
Rule 8 - Sec 1a

If returning to a base during a dead ball,
a runner need not touch in reverse order.

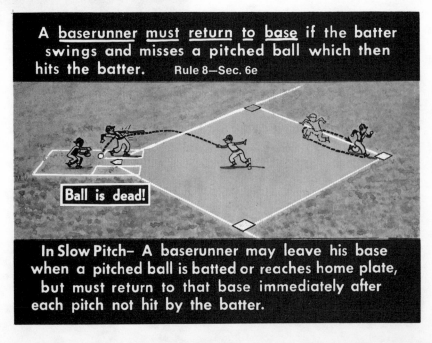

A baserunner must return to base if the batter
swings and misses a pitched ball which then
hits the batter.   Rule 8—Sec. 6e

Ball is dead!

In Slow Pitch– A baserunner may leave his base
when a pitched ball is batted or reaches home plate,
but must return to that base immediately after
each pitch not hit by the batter.

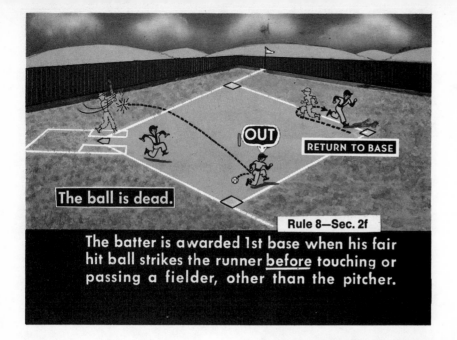

The ball is dead.

RETURN TO BASE

Rule 8—Sec. 2f

The batter is awarded 1st base when his fair hit ball strikes the runner <u>before</u> touching or passing a fielder, other than the pitcher.

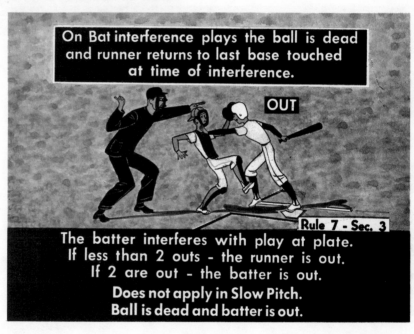

On Bat interference plays the ball is dead and runner returns to last base touched at time of interference.

OUT

Rule 7 - Sec. 3

The batter interferes with play at plate.
If less than 2 outs - the runner is out.
If 2 are out - the batter is out.

**Does not apply in Slow Pitch.
Ball is dead and batter is out.**

When is a baserunner out?

Ball is in play

Rule 8—Sec. 8b

The <u>runner</u> <u>is</u> <u>out</u> when he is tagged
by a fielder while off base.

Ball is alive!

Rule 8—Sec. 8e

The runner is <u>out</u> if he passes the preceding
runner unless that runner has been put out.

Ball is alive.

Could occur at any base

Rule 8—Sec. 8a

The runner is <u>out</u> if he runs <u>outside</u> the
base line to avoid being tagged.

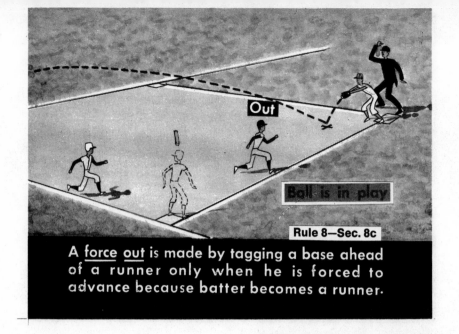

Out

Ball is in play

Rule 8—Sec. 8c

A _force_ _out_ is made by tagging a base ahead of a runner only when he is forced to advance because batter becomes a runner.

An Appeal Play!   Out

Rule 8—Sec. 8g

If a runner misses a base, he may be put out by a fielder touching the base with the ball before the runner retags the base.

An Appeal Play!
Over-ran

Ball is in play

Rule 8—Sec. 8h

Failing to return to 1st base immediately after overrunning or oversliding. However, a runner can turn left in fair territory in returning to base if he does not make a move to advance to 2nd.

This is an appeal play.

Rule 8—Sec. 8f

If a runner leaves base <u>before</u> a fly ball, fair or foul, is touched, he is out if he is tagged before his return to base.

An appeal play

Rule 8—Effect Sec. 8f-i

Ball is in play when an appeal play is enforced and involved.

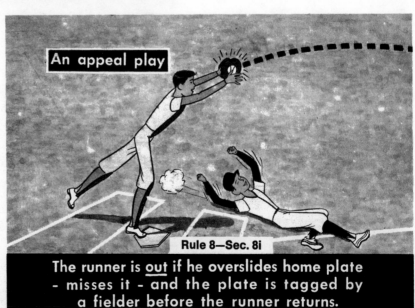

An appeal play

Rule 8—Sec. 8i

The runner is <u>out</u> if he overslides home plate - misses it - and the plate is tagged by a fielder before the runner returns.

INTERFERENCE

The ball is dead.

Rule 9—Sec. 1t
Rule 8—Sec. 8p

The runner is <u>out</u> if teammates gather around a base to which runner is advancing to confuse or hinder the defensive team.

The ball is dead.

Rule 8—Sec. 8j

The runner is <u>out</u> when he intentionally interferes with a thrown ball.

Interference

Ball is dead!

Rule 8—Sec. 8j

The runner is <u>out</u> when he fails to yield right of way to a fielder fielding a fair hit ball.

The ball is dead. | Rule 8—Sec. 8j

If this interference, in the judgment of the umpire, is an obvious attempt to prevent a double play, the immediate succeeding runner shall also be called out.

Ball is dead! | Rule 8—Sec. 8m

A baserunner is <u>out</u> if the coacher bodily assists runner.
Provided <u>a</u> <u>play</u> is <u>being</u> <u>made</u> <u>on</u> <u>him</u>.

OFFICIAL RULES FOR BASERUNNING

(Rule 8)

Sec. 1. THE BASERUNNERS MUST TOUCH BASES IN LEGAL ORDER, I.E., FIRST, SECOND, THIRD AND HOME PLATE.

a. When a baserunner must return while the ball is in play, he must touch the bases in reverse order.
EFFECT—Sec. 1a: The ball is in play and baserunners must return with liability to be put out.

b. When a baserunner acquires the right to a base by touching it before being put out he is entitled to hold the base until he has legally touched the next base in order or is forced to vacate it for a succeeding baserunner.

c. When a baserunner dislodges a base from its proper position neither he nor succeeding runners in the same series of plays are compelled to follow a base unreasonably out of position.
EFFECT—Sec. 1b-c: The ball is in play and baserunners may advance with liability to be put out.

d. A baserunner shall not run bases in reverse order either to confuse the fielders or to make a travesty of the game.
EFFECT—Sec. 1d: The ball is dead and the baserunner is out.

e. Two baserunners may not occupy the same base simultaneously.
EFFECT—Sec. 1e: The runner who first legally occupied the base shall be entitled to it; the other baserunner may be put out by being touched with the ball.

f. Failure of a **preceding** runner to touch a base, or to leave a base legally on a caught fly ball and who is declared out does not affect the status of a **succeeding** baserunner who touches bases in proper order. However, if the failure to touch a base in regular order or to leave a base legally on a caught fly ball, is the third out of the inning **no succeeding** runner may score a run.

g. No runner may return to touch a missed base or one he had left illegally, after a following runner has scored. After the ball becomes dead, no runner may return to touch a missed base or one he has left after he has advanced to and touched a base beyond the missed base or one he has left illegally, even after the ball becomes alive.

h. No runner may return to touch a missed base or one he had left illegally, once he enters his team area.

i. When a walk is issued, all runners must touch all bases in legal order.

j. Bases left too soon on a caught fly ball must be retouched while in route to awarded bases.

k. Awarded bases must also be touched and in proper order.

Sec. 2. THE BATTER BECOMES A BASERUNNER.

a. As soon as he hits a fair ball.
EFFECT—Sec. 2a: The ball is in play and the batter becomes a baserunner with liability to be put out.

b. (FP ONLY) When the catcher fails to catch the third strike before the ball touches the ground when there are less than two outs and first base is unoccupied, or anytime there are two outs. This is called the third strike rule.

c. When a fair ball strikes the person or clothing of an umpire on foul ground.
EFFECT—Sec. 2b-c: The ball is in play and the batter becomes a baserunner with liability to be put out.

d. When four balls have been called by the umpire.
EFFECT—Sec. 2d: (FP) The ball is in play unless it has been blocked. The batter is entitled to one base without liability to be put out.
EFFECT—Sec. 2d: (SP) The ball is dead. Baserunners may not advance unless forced. If the pitcher desires to walk a batter intentionally he may do so by notifying the plate umpire, who shall award the batter first base.

e. When the catcher or any other fielder interferes with or prevents him from striking at a pitched ball.
EFFECT—Sec. 2e: The ball is dead and not in play and the batter is entitled to one base without liability to be put out unless the batter reaches first base safely and all other runners have advanced at least one base then play continues without reference to the interference.

f. When a fair ball strikes the person or clothing of the umpire or a baserunner on fair ground.
EFFECT—Sec. 2f: (1) If the ball hits the umpire or baserunner after passing a fielder other than the pitcher or touched by infielder including the pitcher the ball is in play. (2) If the ball hits the umpire or baserunner before passing

a fielder, the ball is dead and the batter is entitled to first base without liability to be put out.

g. (FP ONLY) When a pitched ball not struck at touches any part of the batter's person or clothing while he is in the batter's box. It does not matter if the ball strikes the ground before hitting him. The batter's hands are not to be considered as part of the bat.
EFFECT—Sec. 2g: The ball is dead and the batter is entitled to one base without liability to be put out unless he made no effort to avoid being hit. In this case, the plate umpire calls either a ball or a strike.

Sec. 3 BASERUNNERS ARE ENTITLED TO ADVANCE WITH LIABILITY TO BE PUT OUT UNDER THE FOLLOWING CIRCUMSTANCES:

a. (FP ONLY) When a ball leaves the pitcher's hand on a pitch.

b. When the ball is overthrown into fair or foul territory and is not blocked.

c. When the ball is batted into fair territory and is not blocked.

d. A legally caught fly ball is first touched.

e. If a fair ball strikes the umpire or a baserunner after having passed an infielder, other than the pitcher or having been touched by an infielder, including the pitcher, the ball shall be considered in play. Also, if a fair ball strikes an umpire on foul ground, the ball shall be in play.
EFFECT—Sec. 3a-e: The ball is alive and in play.

Sec. 4. A PLAYER FORFEITS HIS EXEMPTION FROM LIABILITY TO GET PUT OUT:

a. If while the ball is in play he fails to touch the base to which he was entitled before attempting to make the next base. If the runner put out, is the batter-baserunner at first base or any other baserunner forced to advance because the batter became a baserunner, this out is a force-out.

b. If after overrunning first base, the batter-baserunner attempts to continue to second base.

c. If after dislodging the base, the batter-baserunner tries to continue to the next base.

Sec. 5. BASERUNNERS ARE ENTITLED TO ADVANCE WITHOUT LIABILITY TO BE PUT OUT:

a. When forced to vacate a base because the batter was awarded a base on balls.
EFFECT—Sec. 5a: (FP) The ball remains in play unless it is blocked. Baserunner affected is entitled to one base and may advance further at his own risk if the ball is in play.
EFFECT—Sec. 5a: (SP) The ball is dead.

b. When a fielder obstructs the baserunner from making a base unless the fielder is trying to field a batted ball or has the ball ready to touch the baserunner.
EFFECT—Sec. 5b: When obstruction occurs, the umpire shall call and signal "Obstruction."
(1) If a play is being made on the obstructed runner, or if the batter-runner is obstructed before he touches first base, the ball is dead and all runners shall advance, without liability to be put out, to the bases they would reached, in the umpire's judgment, if there had been no obstruction. The obstructed runner shall be awarded at least one base beyond the base he had last legally touched before the obstruction. Any preceding runners, forced to advance by the award of bases as the penalty for obstruction, shall advance without liability to be put out.
(2) If no play is being made on the obstructed runner, the play shall proceed until no further action is possible. The umpire shall then call "TIME" and impose such penalties, if any, as in his judgment will nullify the act of obstruction.

c. (FP ONLY) When a wild pitch or passed ball goes under, over, through or lodges in the backstop.
EFFECT—Sec. 5c: The ball is dead. All baserunners are awarded one base only. The batter is awarded first base only on the fourth ball.

d. When forced to vacate a base because the batter was awarded a base.
(1) (FP ONLY) For being hit by a pitched ball.

(2) For being interfered with by the catcher when striking at a pitched ball.

(3) (FP ONLY) If, with a runner on third base and trying to score by means of a squeeze play or a steal, the catcher or any other fielder steps on, or in front of home plate without possession of the ball, or touches the batter or his bat, the pitcher shall be charged with an illegal pitch, the batter shall be awarded first base on the interference and regular ball is dead.

EFFECT—Sec. 5d: (1)-(3): The ball is dead and baserunners may not advance farther than the base to which they are entitled.

e. (FP ONLY) When a pitcher makes an illegal pitch.

EFFECT—Sec. 5e: The ball is dead and baserunners may advance to the base to which they are entitled without liability to be put out.

f. When a fielder contacts or catches a fair batted or thrown ball with his cap, mask, glove or any part of his uniform while it is detached from its proper place on his person.

EFFECT—Sec. 5f: The baserunners shall be entitled to 3 bases if a batted ball, or 2 bases if a thrown ball, and in either case the baserunners may advance further at their own risk. If the illegal catch or touch is made on a fair hit ball, which in the opinion of the umpire, would have cleared the outfield fence in flight, the runner shall be awarded a home run.

g. When the ball is in play and is overthrown into foul territory and is blocked.

EFFECT—Sec. 5g: The ball is dead. In all cases where a thrown ball goes into a stand for spectators or over, through or under any fence surrounding the playing field, or hits any person or object not engaged in the game, or into the players' benches (including bats lying near such benches), whether the ball rebounds into the playing field or not, or remains in the meshes of any wire screen protecting the spectators, each and every baserunner shall be awarded 2 bases. When a first throw is made by an infielder, the umpire in awarding such bases shall be governed by the position of each runner at the time the ball was delivered by the pitcher; when the throw is made by an outfielder or is the result of any succeeding play or attempted play; the award shall be governed by the position of each runner and the last base he has touched at the time the final throw was made. In Fast Pitch only, when the throw is made by the catcher on a ball not hit, the award shall be governed by the position of each runner and the last base he has touched at the time of the throw. When a fielder loses possession of the ball such as on an attempted tag, and the ball then enters the dead ball area or becomes blocked, all runners are awarded 1 base from the last base touched at the time the ball entered the dead ball area or became blocked.

NOTE: If all runners, including the batter-runner have advanced at least 1 base when an infielder makes a wild throw on the first play after the pitch, the award shall be governed by the position of the runners when the wild throw was made.

h. When a fair-batted fly ball goes over the fence or into the stands it shall entitle the batter to a home run unless it passes out of the grounds or into a distance less than 225 feet (74.25 m) (Male & Female Fast Pitch), 250 feet (82.5 m) (Female Slow Pitch), or 275 feet (90.75 m) (Male Slow Pitch) from home plate, in which case the batter shall be entitled to 2 bases only. The batter must touch the bases in regular order. The point at which the fence or stand is less than 225 feet (74.25 m) (Male & Female Fast Pitch), 250 feet (82.5 m) (Female Slow Pitch) or 275 feet (90.75 m) (Male Slow Pitch) from home plate shall be plainly indicated for the umpire's guidance.

i. When a fair ball bounds or rolls into a stand, over, under, or through a fence or other obstruction marking the boundaries of the playing field.

EFFECT—Sec. 5i: The ball is dead and all baserunners are awarded 2 bases, from time of pitch.

j. When a legally caught ball in playable territory is carried by the fielder unintentionally into dead ball territory, the ball is dead, the batter is out and all runners advance 1 base beyond the base they occupied at the time of the pitch. If, in the judgment of the umpire, the fielder INTENTIONALLY carries a legally caught fly ball into dead ball territory, the ball is dead, the batter is out and all runners are awarded 2 bases beyond the base they occupied at the time of the pitch.

Sec. 6. A BASERUNNER MUST RETURN TO HIS BASE UNDER THE FOLLOWING CIRCUMSTANCES:

a. When a foul ball is illegally caught and is so declared by the umpire.

b. When an illegally batted ball is declared by the umpire.

c. When a batter or baserunner is called out for interference. Other baserunners shall return to the last base which was in the judgment of the umpire legally touched by him at the time of the interference.

d. (FP ONLY) When there is interference by the plate umpire or his clothing with the catcher's attempt to throw.

e. When any part of the batter's person is touched by a pitched ball swung at and missed.

f. When a batter is hit by a pitched ball, unless forced.

g. When a foul ball is not caught.

EFFECT—Sec. 6a-g: (1) The ball is dead. (2) The baserunners must return to base without liability to be put out except when forced to go to the next base because the batter became a baserunner. (3) No runs shall score unless all bases are occupied. (4) Baserunners need not touch the intervening bases in returning to base but must return promptly. (5) However, they must be allowed sufficient time to return.

h. (SP ONLY) Base Stealing. Under no conditions is a runner permitted to steal a base when a pitched ball is not batted. The runner must return to his base.

EFFECT—Sec. 6h: Baserunners may leave their base when a pitched ball is batted or reaches home plate, but must return to that base immediately after each pitch not hit by the batter.

i. When a caught fair fly ball (including a line drive) (FP & SP) or bunt (FP ONLY) which can be caught by an infielder with ordinary effort is intentionally dropped with less than 2 outs, with a runner on 1st base, 1st & 2nd, 1st & 3rd or 1st, 2nd and 3rd base.

Sec. 7. BATTER-BASERUNNERS ARE OUT UNDER THE FOLLOWING CIRCUMSTANCES:

a. (FP ONLY) When the catcher drops the third strike and he is legally touched with the ball by a fielder before touching first base.

b. (FP ONLY) When the catcher drops the third strike and the ball is held on first base before the batter-runner reaches first base.

c. When after a fair ball is hit, he is legally touched with the ball before he touches first base.

d. When after a fair ball, the ball is held by a fielder touching first base with any part of his person before the batter-baserunner touches first base.

e. When after a fly ball is caught by a fielder before it touches the ground or any object other than a fielder.

f. When after a ball is hit or a base on balls is issued, or when the batter may legally advance to 1st base on a dropped 3rd strike (FP ONLY), he fails to advance to 1st base and instead enters his team area.

EFFECT—Sec. 7a-f: The ball is in play and the batter-baserunner is out.

g. When he runs outside the 3-foot (0.99 m) line and in the opinion of the umpire interferes with the fielder taking the throw at first base. However, he may run outside the 3-foot (0.99m) line to avoid a fielder attempting to field a batted ball.

h. When he interferes with a fielder attempting to field a batted ball or intentionally interferes with a thrown ball. If this interference, in the judgment of the umpire, is an obvious attempt to prevent a double play, the baserunner closest to home plate shall also be called out.

i. When a batter baserunner interferes with a play at home plate in an attempt to prevent an obvious out at the plate. The runner is also out.

EFFECT—Sec. 7 g-i: The ball is dead and the batter-baserunner is out.

Sec. 8. THE BASERUNNER IS OUT:

a. When in running to any base, he runs more than 3 feet (0.99 m) from a direct line between a base and the next one in regular or reverse order to avoid being touched by the ball in the hand of a fielder.

b. When, while the ball is in play, he is legally touched with the ball in the hand of a fielder while not in contact with a base.

c. When on a force-out a fielder tags him with the ball or holds the ball on the base to which the baserunner is forced to advance before the runner reaches the base.

d. When the baserunner fails to return to touch the base he previously occupied when play is resumed after suspension of play.

e. When a baserunner physically passes a preceding baserunner before that runner has been put out.
EFFECT—Sec. 8a-e: The ball is in play and the baserunner is out.
f. When the baserunner leaves his base to advance to another base before a caught fly ball has touched a fielder, provided the ball is returned to a fielder and legally held on that base or a fielder legally touches the baserunner before the baserunner returns to his base.
g. When the baserunner fails to touch the intervening base or bases in regular or reverse order and the ball is in play and legally held on that base, or the baserunner is legally touched while off the base that he missed.
h. When the batter-runner legally overruns first base, attempts to run to second base and is legally touched while off base.
i. In running or sliding for home base, he fails to touch home base and makes no attempt to return to the base, when a fielder holds the ball in his hand while touching home base, and appeals to the umpire for the decision.
EFFECT—Sec. 8f-i: (1) These are appeal plays and the defensive team loses the privilege of putting the baserunner out if the appeal is not made before the next pitch, legal or illegal. (2) The ball is in play and the base runner is out.
NOTE On appeal plays, the appeal must be made before the next pitch, legal or illegal, or before the defensive team has left the field. The defensive team has "left the field" when the pitcher and all infielders have clearly left their normal fielding positions and have left fair territory on their way to the bench or dugout area. (3) Baserunners may leave their base on appeal plays when:
(a) (FP ONLY) The ball leaves the 8 foot (2.64 m) circle around the pitcher's plate or when the ball leaves the pitcher's possession.
(b) (SP ONLY) The defensive team makes known their intent to appeal or the pitcher steps backwards off the pitcher's plate or throws the ball while off the pitcher's plate and after the umpire declares "Play Ball."
j. When the baserunner interferes with a fielder attempting to field a batted ball or intentionally interferes with a thrown ball. If this interference, in the judgment of the umpire, is an obvious attempt to prevent a double play, the immediate succeeding runner shall also be called out.
k. When a baserunner is struck with a fair batted ball while off base and before it passes an infielder excluding the pitcher.
l. When a runner intentionally kicks a ball which an infielder has missed.
m. When a baserunner on third base, the batter interferes with a play being made at home plate with less than 2 outs.
n. When in the judgment of the umpire, the base coach at third base or first base, touches or holds the runner, physically to assist this runner in returning to or leaving third or first base. The runner is not out if a play is not being made on him.
o. When the coach near third base runs in the direction of home plate on or near the baseline while a fielder is attempting to make a play on a batted or thrown ball and thereby draws a throw to home plate. The baserunner nearest to third base shall be declared out.
p. When one or more members of the offensive team stand or collect at or around a base to which a baserunner is advancing thereby confusing the fielders and adding to the difficulty of making the play.
NOTE: Sec. 8p: Members of a team includes bat boy or any other person authorized to sit on team's bench.
q. When the baserunner runs the bases in reverse order, to confuse the defensive team or to make a farce out of the game. This includes the batter-runner moving back toward home plate to avoid or delay a tag by a fielder.
r. If coach intentionally interferes with a thrown ball.
When a runner, after being declared out or after scoring, interferes with a defensive player's opportunity to make a play on another runner, the runner closest to home plate at the time of the interference, shall be declared out.
EFFECT—Sec. 8j-s: The ball is dead and the baserunner is out. No bases may be run unless necessitated by the batter becoming a baserunner.
t. (FP ONLY) When the baserunner fails to keep contact with the base to which he is entitled until a legally pitched ball has been released. When a baserunner is legitimately off his base after a pitch or the result of a batter completing his turn at bat, while the pitcher has the ball within an 8 foot (2.64 m) radius of the pitcher's plate, he must immediately attempt to advance to the next base or immediately return to his base.
(1) Failure to immediately proceed to the next base or return to his base, once the pitcher has the ball within the 8 foot (2.64 m) radius of the pitcher's plate, shall result in the baserunner being declared out.
(2) Once the runner returns to a base, for any reason he shall be declared out if he leaves said base unless a play is made on him or another runner; or the pitcher does not have the ball in the 8 foot (2.64m) radius; or the pitcher released the ball to the batter.
NOTE: A base on balls or dropped 3rd strike in which the runner is entitled to run, is treated the same as a batted ball. The batter-runner may continue past first base, and is entitled to run toward second base, as long as he does not stop at first base. If he stops after he rounds first base he then must comply with Section 8t (1).
u. (SP ONLY) When the baserunner fails to keep contact with the base to which he is entitled, until a legally pitched ball has reached home plate.
EFFECT—Sec. 8t-u: The ball is dead. NO PITCH is declared and the baserunner is out.

Sec. 9. BASERUNNERS ARE NOT OUT UNDER THE FOLLOWING CIRCUMSTANCES:
a. When a baserunner runs behind the fielder and outside the baseline in order to avoid interfering with a fielder attempting to field the ball in the base path.
b. When a baserunner does not run in a direct line to the base providing the fielder in the direct line does not have the ball in his possession.
c. When more than one fielder attempts to field a batted ball and the baserunner comes in contact with the one who, in the umpire's judgment, was not entitled to field the ball.
d. When a baserunner is hit with a fair batted ball that has passed through an infielder, excluding the pitcher, and in the umpire's judgment no other infielder had a chance to play the ball.
e. When a baserunner is touched with a ball not securely held by a fielder.
f. When the defensive team does not request the umpire's decision on an appeal play until after the next pitch.
g. When the batter-runner overruns first base after touching it and returning directly to the base.
h. When the baserunner is not given sufficient time to return to a base, he shall not be called out for being off base before the pitcher releases the ball. He may advance as though he had left the base legally.
i. A runner who has legally started to advance cannot be stopped by the pitcher receiving the ball while on the pitching plate nor by stepping on the plate with the ball in his possession.
j. When a baserunner holds his base until a fly ball touches a fielder and then attempts to advance.
k. When hit by a batted ball when touching their base, unless they intentionally interfere with the ball or a fielder making a play.
l. When a baserunner slides into a base and dislodges it from its proper position, the base is considered to have followed the runner.
EFFECT—Sec. 9l: A baserunner having made such a base safely shall not be out for being off that base. He may return to that base without liability to be put out when the base has been replaced. A runner forfeits this exemption if he attempts to advance beyond the dislodged base before it is again in proper position.
m. When a fielder makes a play on a runner while using an illegal glove. The manager of the offended team has the option of having the entire play, including the batter's turn at bat, nullified, with the batter batting over, assuming the ball and strike count he had before he hit the ball and runners returned to their original bases which they held prior to the batted ball or taking the result of the play.
n. When the baserunner is hit by a fair batted ball, after it is touched or touches any fielder, including the pitcher.

OFFICIAL RULES FOR
DEAD BALL AND BALL IN PLAY

(Rule 9)

Sec. 1. THE BALL IS DEAD AND NOT IN PLAY IN THE FOLLOWING CIRCUMSTANCES:

a. When the ball is batted illegally.

b. When the batter steps from one box to another when the pitcher is ready to pitch.

c. When a ball is pitched illegally.
EXCEPTION—Sec. 1c: (FP) If the pitcher completes the delivery of the ball to the batter and the batter hits the ball, reaches first safely and all baserunners advance at least one base, then the play stands and the pitch is no longer illegal.
EXCEPTION—Sec. 1c: (SP) If the batter swing at an illegal pitch, the play stands and the pitch is no longer illegal.

d. When "No Pitch" is declared.

e. When a pitched ball touches any part of the batter's person or clothing whether the ball is struck at or not.

f. When a foul ball is not caught.

g. When a baserunner is called out for leaving the base too soon on a pitched ball.

h. When the offensive team causes an interference.
(1) When a batter intentionally strikes the ball a second time, strikes it with a thrown bat, or deflects its course in any way while running to first base.
(2) When an overthrow is intentionally touched by a coach.
(3) When a fair ball strikes a baserunner or umpire before touching an infielder including the pitcher or before passing an infielder other than the pitcher.
(4) When the batter interferes with the catcher.
(5) When a member of the offensive team interferes intentionally with a live ball.
(6) When a runner intentionally kicks a ball which a fielder has missed.
(7) (FP ONLY) When, with a baserunner on third base, the batter interferes with the play being made at home plate with less than two outs.

i. The ball shall not be playable outside the established limits of the playing field.

j. If an accident to a runner is such as to prevent him from proceeding to a base to which he is awarded, a substitute runner shall be permitted for the injured player.

k. In case of interference with batter or fielder.

l. (SP ONLY) When the batter bunts or chops the pitched ball.

m. (FP ONLY) When a wild pitch or passed ball goes under, over or through the backstop.

n. When time is called by the umpire.

o. When any part of the batter's person is hit with his own batted ball when he is in the batter's box.

p. When a baserunner runs bases in reverse order either to confuse the fielders or to make a travesty of the game.

q. When the batter is hit by a pitched ball.

r. When in the judgment of the umpire, the coach touches or helps the runner physically to assist him to return or to leave a base or when the coach near third base runs in the direction of home plate on or near the baseline while the fielder is attempting to make a play on a batted or thrown ball and thereby draws a throw to home plate.

s. (FP ONLY) When there is interference by the plate umpire or his clothing with the catcher's attempt to throw.

t. When one or more members of the offensive team stand or collect at or around a base to which a baserunner is advancing, thereby confusing the fielders and adding to the difficulty of making a play.

u. (FP ONLY) When the baserunner fails to keep contact with the base to which he is entitled, until a legally pitched ball has been released.

v. (SP ONLY) When a baserunner fails to keep contact with the base to which he is entitled, until a legally pitched ball has reached home plate.

w. When a play is being made on an obstructed runner or if the batter-runner is obstructed before he touches first base.

x. (SP ONLY) After each strike or ball.

y. When the catcher interferes with the batter's attempt to hit a pitch.
EXCEPTION—Sec. 1y: The ball remains alive if the batter reaches first base safely and all other runners have advanced at least one base.

z. When a blocked ball is declared.

aa. When a batter enters the batter's box with or uses an altered bat.

ab. When a batter hits a ball with an illegal bat.

ac. When a caught fair fly ball (including a line drive) (FP & SP) or bunt (FP ONLY) which can be handled by an infielder with ordinary effort is intentionally dropped with less than 2 outs and a runner on 1st base, 1st & 2nd, 1st & 3rd or 1st, 2nd, and 3rd base.

ad. When a fielder intentionally carries a legally caught fly ball into dead ball
EFFECT—Sec. 1a-1ad: Baserunners cannot advance on a dead ball, unless forced to do so by reason of the batter having reached first base as entitled to or they are awarded a base or bases.

Sec. 2. THE BALL IS IN PLAY IN THE FOLLOWING CIRCUMSTANCES:

a. At the start of the game and each half inning when the pitcher has the ball while standing in his pitching position and the plate umpire has called "Play Ball."

b. When the ball becomes dead, it shall be put in play when the pitcher is within 8 feet (2.64 m) of the pitcher's plate with the ball and the plate umpire calls "Play Ball."

c. When the infield fly rule is enforced.

d. When a thrown ball goes past a fielder and remains in playable territory.

e. When a fair ball strikes an umpire or baserunner on fair ground after passing or touching an infielder.

f. When a fair ball strikes an umpire on foul ground.

g. When the baserunners have reached the bases to which they are entitled when the fielder illegally fields a batted or thrown ball.

h. When a baserunner is called out for passing a preceding runner.

i. When no play is being made on an obstructed runner, the ball shall remain alive until the play is over.

j. When a fair ball is legally batted.

k. When a baserunner must return in reverse order while the ball is in play.

l. When a baserunner acquires the right to a base by touching it before being put out.

m. When a base is dislodged while baserunners are progressing around the bases.

n. When a baserunner runs more than 3 feet (0.99 m) from a direct line between a base and the next one in regular or reverse order to avoid being touched by the ball in the hand of a fielder.

o. When a baserunner is tagged or forced out.

p. When the umpire calls the baserunner out for failure to return and touch the base when play is resumed after a suspension of play.

q. When an appeal play is enforced and involved.

r. When the batter hits the ball.

s. When a live ball strikes a photographer, groundskeeper, policeman, etc., assigned to the game.

t. When a fly ball has been legally caught.

u. When a thrown ball goes into foul territory and is neither blocked nor obstructed.

v. When a thrown ball strikes an offensive player.

w. If the batter drops the bat and the ball rolls against the bat in fair territory and, in the umpire's judgment, there was no intention to interfere with the course of the ball, the batter is not out and the ball is alive and in play.

x. When a thrown ball strikes an umpire.

y. Whenever the ball is not dead as provided in Section 1 of this rule.

z. When a thrown ball strikes a coach.

aa. (FP ONLY) When a ball has been called on the batter and when four balls have been called but the batter may not be put out before he reaches first base.

ab. (FP ONLY) When a strike has been called on the batter and when three strikes have been called on the batter.

ac. (FP ONLY) When a foul tip has been legally caught.

ad. (SP ONLY) As long as there is a play as a result of the hit by the batter. This includes a subsequent appeal play.

ae. (FP ONLY) If the ball slips from a pitcher's hand during his wind-up or during the back swing.

Sec.3. (SP ONLY) THE BALL REMAINS ALIVE UNTIL THE UMPIRE CALLS "TIME" WHICH SHOULD BE DONE WHEN THE BALL IS HELD BY A PLAYER IN THE INFIELD AREA AND IN THE OPINION OF THE UMPIRE, ALL PLAY HAS CEASED.

THE UMPIRE

When players concentrate on playing and managers on managing, umpires can concentrate on umpiring, making the game more enjoyable for all concerned. Umpiring is a challenge, but there is real satisfaction in doing a difficult job and performing an essential service for the boys who gain much through playing the game.

UMPIRES PLAY IMPORTANT PART

Umpires have a right to ask for and to receive the cooperation and respect of the managers, coaches, players and spectators.

It is natural that any close play will bring divided opinions, but everyone must keep in mind that the umpire is a neutral observer able to judge a play from a neutral viewpoint.

Some of the Duties of the Umpire before the Game Begins.

The umpire arrives early to inspect playing field.
See that the field is marked plainly.

See that pitcher's plate is in good condition.

Be sure the foul posts are up.

The umpire inspects equipment.

Receive batting orders in duplicate. Check
to be sure they are identical. Give extra
copy to opposing manager.

DURING THE GAME

Officials have an excellent opportunity to build sportsmanship and create constructive attitudes in all of the players.

Umpires:

- know the rules.
- are in the proper positions to call the plays.
- are alert for the unexpected development.
- can keep their feelings under control and remain non-partisan in all situations.
- call the plays as they see them.
- are performing a friendly service - - which is essential to the game.

Once the game has started, the umpire has complete charge and has the authority to make decisions not specifically covered by the rules.

"Play Ball" is the term used by the plate umpire to indicate that play shall begin or be resumed.

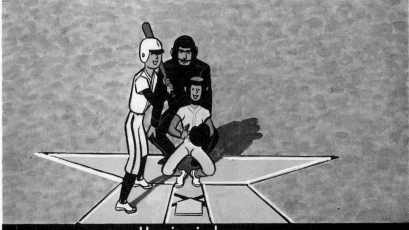

Umpire judges balls and strikes over catcher's shoulder nearer batter.

When there is <u>one</u> umpire, <u>he</u> <u>remains</u> <u>behind</u> the plate until the pitch is delivered.

On other than tag plays, "Listen" for the ball to hit the glove.

"Look" for tag of runner's foot and also try to catch ball out of corner of your eye.

Be in a position to see every play.

On any force play, "listen" for the ball to hit the glove.

KEEP YOUR EYE ON THE BALL.   HUSTLE

Be in a position to see every play.

Protect yourself on an infield fly. Always call "Infield fly if fair" when the ball is near the foul line.

KEEP YOUR EYE ON THE BALL.   HUSTLE

Verbal calls on foul balls!

Fair or Foul Balls - Indicate by hand signals pointing _inside_ foul lines for a _fair ball_ and _outside_ foul lines for a _foul ball_.

When anyone questions decision, give friendly explanation of reason for decision. Then call for resumption of play. "Let's play ball."

When anyone argues, listen briefly, say "I saw the play this way and that's it. Play ball." Then walk a few steps away.

To avoid arguments between innings, go to side opposite team going to field.

Don't "give away" appeal plays. Act as if nothing wrong had occurred.

A baserunner is out if the umpire
upholds an appeal play.

Plate umpire
All batting substitutions should be reported
to the umpire.

All fielding substitutions should be reported
to the umpire.

When cleaning home plate, step inside the diamond, face crowd, turn back to pitcher, lean over and brush plate. Keep plate clean.

Rule 5 - Sec. 3 c

It is the duty of the Umpire to stop the game when it is no longer safe to play.

Be in a position to see every play.

The umpire's signal for safe.

The Most Common Signals Are:

Be in a position to see every play.

OUT!

The umpire's signal for out.

Keep your eye on the ball.

STRIKE ONE!

The umpire's signal for a strike.

The umpire's signal for a strike.

Give balls on left hand, strikes on right hand every few pitches. It avoids unnecessary questions.

"Balls" are not indicated, merely called vocally.

The umpire's signal for time out.

OFFICIAL RULES FOR UMPIRES

(Rule 10)

Sec. 1. POWER AND DUTIES. The umpires are the representatives of the league or organization by which they have been assigned to a particular game, and as such are authorized and required to enforce each section of these rules. They have the power to order a player, coach, captain or manager to do or omit to do any act which in their judgment is necessary to give force and effect to one or all of these rules and to inflict penalties as herein prescribed. The plate umpire shall have the authority to make decisions on any situations not specifically covered in the rules.

GENERAL INFORMATION FOR UMPIRES

1. The umpire shall not be a member of either team. Examples: (player, coach, manager, officer, scorer or sponsor.)
2. The umpires should be sure of the date, time and place for the game and should arrive at the playing field 20-30 minutes ahead of time, start the game on time and leave the field when the game is over.
3. Male umpires shall wear a powder blue shirt, long or short sleeves, and dark navy blue trousers and cap. Female umpires shall wear a powder blue blouse, long or short sleeves and dark navy blue, full length, slacks. A cap is not required for female umpires. All other paraphernalia such as socks, belt, ball bag and jacket must also be dark navy blue for both male and female umpires. Both male and female umpires working behind the plate in Fast Pitch MUST wear a mask. It is recommended that they wear a mask behind the plate in Slow Pitch also. Female umpires working behind the plate in Fast Pitch MUST wear a body protector. It is recommended that female umpires working behind the plate in Slow Pitch also wear a body protector.
4. The umpires should introduce themselves to the captains, managers and scorer.
5. The umpires should inspect the playing field boundaries, equipment and clarify all ground rules to both teams and their coaches.
6. Each umpire shall have the power to make decisions on violations committed any time during playing time or during suspension of play until the game is over.
7. Neither umpire has the authority to set aside or question decisions made by the other within the limits of their respective duties as outlined in these rules.
8. An umpire may consult his associate at any time. However, the final decision shall rest with the umpire whose exclusive authority it was to make the decision and who requested the opinion of the other.
9. In order to define their respective duties, the umpire judging balls and strikes shall be designated as the "Plate Umpire," the umpire judging base decisions as the "Base Umpire."
10. The plate umpire or base umpire shall have equal authority to:
    (a) Call a runner out for leaving a base too soon.
    (b) Call TIME for suspension of play.
    (c) Remove a player, coach or manager from the game for violation of rules.
    (d) Call all illegal pitches.
11. The umpire shall declare the batter or baserunner out without waiting for an appeal for such decision in all cases where such player is retired in accordance with these rules.
    NOTE: Unless appealed to, the umpire does not call a player out for having failed to touch base, leaving a base too soon on a fly ball, batting out of order, or making an attempt to go to second after reaching first base, as provided in these rules.
12. Umpires shall not penalize a team for infraction of a rule when imposing the penalty would be to the advantage of the offending team.
13. Failure of umpires to adhere to Rule 10 shall not be grounds for protest. These are guidelines for umpires.

Sec. 2. THE PLATE UMPIRE:
a. He shall take a position back of the catcher. He shall have full charge of and be responsible for the proper conduct of the game.
b. He shall call all balls and strikes.
c. He shall by agreement and in cooperation with the base umpire call plays, hit balls, fair or foul, legal or illegal caught balls. On plays which would necessitate the base umpire leaving the infield, the plate umpire shall assume the duties normally required of the base umpire.
d. He shall determine and declare whether:
    (1) A batter bunts or chops a ball.
    (2) A batted ball touches the person or clothing of the batter.
    (3) A fly ball is an infield or an outfield fly.
e. He shall render base decisions as indicated in the umpire's manual.
f. He shall determine when a game is forfeited.
g. He shall assume all duties when assigned as a single umpire to a game.

Sec. 3. THE BASE UMPIRE:
a. He shall take such positions on the playing field as outlined in the umpire's manual.
b. He shall assist the plate umpire in every way to enforce the rules of the game.

Sec. 4. RESPONSIBILITIES OF A SINGLE UMPIRE.
If only one umpire is assigned, his duties and jurisdiction shall extend to all points. He shall take a position in any part of the field which in his judgment will best enable him to discharge his duties.

Sec. 5. CHANGE OF UMPIRES. Umpires cannot be changed during a game by the consent of the opposing teams unless an umpire is incapacitated by injury or illness.

Sec. 6. UMPIRE'S JUDGMENT. There shall be no appeal from any decision of either umpire on the ground that he was not correct in his conclusion as to whether a batted ball was fair or foul, a baserunner safe or out, a pitched ball a strike or ball, or on any play involving accuracy of judgment, and no deicsion rendered by either umpire shall be reversed except that he be convinced it is in violation of one of these rules. In case the manager, captain or either team does seek a reversal of a decision based solely on a point of rules, the umpire whose decision is in question shall, if in doubt, confer with his associate before taking any action. But under no circumstances shall any player or person other than the manager or the captain of either team have any legal right to protest on any decision and seek its reversal on a claim that it is in conflict with these rules.

Under no circumstances shall either umpire seek to reverse a decision made by his associate, nor shall either umpire criticize or interfere with the duties of his associate unless asked to do so by him.

Sec. 7. SIGNALS.
a. To indicate that play shall begin or be resumed the umpire shall call "PLAY BALL" and at the same time motion the pitcher to deliver the ball.
b. To indicate a strike, the umpire shall raise his right hand upward, indicate the number of strikes by the fingers, at the same time calling "STRIKE" in a clear and decisive voice, followed by calling the number of the strike.
c. To indicate ball, no arm signal is used. The call is "BALL" followed by the number of the ball.
d. To indicate the total count of balls and strikes, the balls are called first.
e. To indicate a foul, the umpire shall call "FOUL BALL" and extend his arm horizontally away from the diamond according to the direction of the ball.
f. To indicate a fair ball, the umpire shall extend his arm toward the center of the diamond using a pumping motion.
g. To indicate a batter or baserunner OUT, the umpire shall raise his right hand upward above his right shoulder with fingers closed.
h. To indicate that a player is SAFE, the umpire shall extend both arms diagonally in front of the body with palms toward the ground.
i. To indicate suspension of play, the umpire shall call "TIME" and at the same time extend both arms above his head. The other umpire shall immediately acknowledge the suspension of play with similar action.
j. A delayed dead ball will be signified by the umpire extending his left arm horizontally.
k. To indicate a TRAPPED BALL, the umpire shall extend both arms diagonally in front of the body with palms toward the ground.
l. To indicate GROUND RULE DOUBLE, the umpire shall extend his right hand above his head and indicate with two fingers the number of bases awarded.
m. To indicate HOME RUN, the umpire shall extend his right hand with closed fingers above his head and circle arm in clock-wise movement.
n. To indicate an INFIELD FLY, the umpire shall call "INFIELD FLY, IF FAIR, THE BATTER IS OUT". The umpire shall extend one arm above the head.

Sec. 8. SUSPENSION OF PLAY.
a. An umpire may suspend play when in his judgment conditions justify such action.
b. Play shall be suspended whenever the plate umpire leaves his position to brush the plate or to perform other duties not directly connected with the calling of plays.
c. The umpire shall suspend play whenever a batter or pitcher steps out of position for a legitimate reason.
d. An umpire shall not call TIME after pitcher has started his windup.
e. An umpire shall not call TIME while any play is in progress.
f. In case of injury, TIME shall not be called until all plays in progress have been completed or runners have been held at their bases.
g. Umpires shall not suspend play at the request of players, coaches or managers until all action in progress by either team has been completed.
h. (SP ONLY)When in the opinion of an umpire all immediate play is apparently completed, he should call "TIME".

Sec. 9. VIOLATIONS AND PENALTY.
a. Players, coaches or managers shall not make disparaging or insulting remarks to or about opposing players, officials or spectators.
b. There shall be no more than two coaches for each team to give words of assistance and direction to the members of their team while at bat. One shall be stationed near first base and one near third base and they must remain in the coach's box.
c. The penalty for violations by a player is prompt removal of the offender from the game and grounds. For the first offense, coach or manager may be warned, but for the second offense, they are removed from the game. The offender shall go directly to the dressing room for the remainder of the game or leave the grounds. Failure to do so will warrant a forfeiture of the game.

Positioning of Umpires

Remain outside foul line, not astride line.

Most amateur games use two umpires. One is always behind the plate. With nobody on base the umpire stands as shown.

With two umpires, plate umpire watches lead runner if more than one runner on tag.

Two Umpires - Runner on 1st.

Two Umpires - Runner on 2nd.

Two Umpires - Runner on 3rd.

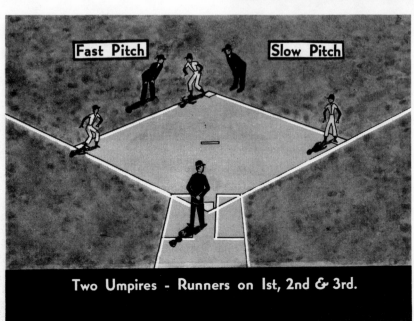

Two Umpires - Runners on 1st, 2nd & 3rd.

Two Umpires - Runners on 1st & 2nd.

Two Umpires - Runners on 2nd & 3rd.

Two Umpires - Runners on 1st & 3rd.

Fundamentals:
1. Be ahead of runners.
2. Move clockwise.
3. Don't back-track, continue clockwise.

Three Umpires - Runner on 1st

Three Umpires - Runner on 2nd.

Three Umpires - Runner on 3rd.

Three Umpires - Runners on 1st, 2nd & 3rd.

Three Umpires - Runners on 1st & 2nd.

Three Umpires - Runners on 1st & 3rd.

Three Umpires - Runners on 2nd & 3rd.

Always remember to thank the officials
after every game

THE UMPIRE

The volunteer umpire deserves the thanks and support of everyone in the program. Even the most conscientious umpire (being human) may make an occasional mistake, but criticism won't correct it anymore than it will an error in judgment by a manager or an error in fielding by a player.

The End